A.W. TOZER

Compiled and Edited by James L. Snyder

THE CRUCIFIED LIFE

HOW TO LIVE OUT A DEEPER CHRISTIAN EXPERIENCE

Regal

From Gospel Light
Ventura, California, U.S.A.

Published by Regal
From Gospel Light
Ventura, California, U.S.A.
www.regalbooks.com
Printed in the U.S.A.

All Scripture quotations, unless otherwise indicated are taken from
the *King James Version*. Authorized King James Version.

Other version used is *NIV*—Scripture taken from the *Holy Bible, New International
Version*®. Copyright © 1973, 1978, 1984, 2010 by International Bible Society.
Used by permission of Zondervan Publishing House. All rights reserved

© 2011 James L. Snyder.
All rights reserved.

Library of Congress Cataloging-in-Publication Data
Tozer, A. W. (Aiden Wilson), 1897-1963.
The crucified life / A. W. Tozer; compiled and edited by James L. Snyder.
p. cm.
ISBN 978-0-8307-5922-4 (trade paper)
1. Christian life—Christian and Missionary Alliance authors.
I. Snyder, James L. II. Title.
BV4501.3.T697 2011
248.4'899—dc23
2011025860

Rights for publishing this book outside the U.S.A. or in non-English languages are
administered by Gospel Light Worldwide, an international not-for-profit ministry.
For additional information, please visit www.glww.org, email info@glww.org, or write
to Gospel Light Worldwide, 1957 Eastman Avenue, Ventura, CA 93003, U.S.A.

To order copies of this book and other Regal products in bulk quantities,
please contact us at 1-800-446-7735.

CONTENTS

Introduction: A Different Way of Living 5

Part I: The Foundation of the Crucified Life

1. The Importance of the Crucified Life 13
2. The Foundation of the Christian Experience 23
3. The Resurrection Side of the Cross 35
4. The Loneliness of the Crucified Life 45

Part II: The Dynamics of the Crucified Life

5. The Case for Going On into the Promised Land 61
6. A Discontent with the Status Quo 75
7. Breaking the Static Condition and Going On 89
8. The Great Obstacle to Living the Crucified Life 101

Part III: The Perils of the Crucified Life

9. The Currency of the Crucified Life 115
10. The Veils that Obscure God's Face 127
11. The Strange Ingenuity of the Christian 137
12. Allowing God to Be Himself 145

Part IV: The Blessings of the Crucified Life

13. The Beauty of Contradictions 157
14. The Refreshment of a Revival 167
15. The Everlasting Rewards of Living the Crucified Life . .179
16. Spiritual Guides for the Journey 189

Conclusion: The Purpose of the Refiner's Fire in the
    Crucified Life 199
Excerpts from *Inspired by Tozer* 211

A Different Way of Living

Some dates are so pivotal that they change the whole course of history. Unfortunately, many of those dates lie comfortably in the shadows of obscurity. One such date in the life of A. W. Tozer has eluded me.

As the story is told, Tozer, a pastor at the time, was visiting one of his favorite bookstores in downtown Chicago. As he was perusing the shelves of used books that were so familiar to him, he ran across an old book that he had never seen before. He purchased the book and took it home, and his life was never the same.

The name of the book was *Spiritual Counsel,* and its author, François Fénelon, struck a warm cord in Tozer's own heart. Although Tozer allowed others to borrow many books in his personal library, he never allowed this one particular book to leave his possession to the day he died. He talked about the book so much that people began to inquire about it. As far as Tozer could determine, the book was out of print, and no other copies were available. One man was so interested in the book that, though Tozer did not allow him to take it out of his library, he did allow him to come and type out chapter after chapter. Such was the prominence that Tozer gave to this book. Much to Tozer's delight, the book was eventually republished in an updated and expanded edition titled *Christian Perfection.*

When you read Fénelon's book, you soon recognize a heartbeat that was also shared by Tozer. No two people were more alike in the spiritual realm. In fact, Fénelon's work so inspired Tozer that if you listen carefully to his sermons, you can hear the words of François Fénelon peek through on many occasions. Tozer, of course, was familiar with the works of other great writes—A. B. Simpson, John Wesley and Andrew Murray to name a few—but something about François Fénelon stirred the depths of his heart and his passion for God.

Fénelon's book introduced Tozer to a whole line of Christian "mystics"—a word not highly acceptable in evangelistic circles during Tozer's time (or even during our own)—and he went on to introduce these mystics to the evangelical church of his time. Tozer was not so much interested in literature as he was in pursuing God, and if an author could open up his heart to more of God, he was interested in that person. As you read this book, you will find many of these old saints of God that stirred Tozer's imagination popping in and out, enriching the message that was so important to him.

During his younger years, Tozer was primarily an evangelist. Although he was also a pastor of a local church, he spent much of his time going around the country preaching in conferences and at churches and camp meetings. His primary message at the time was evangelistic. However, after he encountered François Fénelon, his message began to change. When we come to Tozer in this book, we are coming to a man who is aflame with the message of the crucified life.

The Crucified Life and Spiritual Perfection

Now, what did Tozer mean by the "crucified life"? This entire book is an answer to that question, but here we can simply say that it is the life Christ ransomed on the cross, redeemed from the judgment of sin, and made a worthy and acceptable sacrifice unto God. This represents a quality of life that is far above anything that is natural. It is altogether spiritual, which is a result of a dynamic inspiration from on high.

Another term that was not common among the evangelicals of Tozer's day was "spiritual perfection." This term came from François Fénelon, and it embodied the passion of Tozer's heart. Tozer was quick to point out that he wanted nothing whatsoever to do with anything that did not have biblical authority—and he also threw out anything that was extra-biblical. However, spiritual perfection was a term that Tozer found to be biblical, as Paul writes in Philippians 3:12: "Not as though I had already attained, either were already perfect: but I follow after, if that I may apprehend that for which also I am apprehended of Christ Jesus." This should be the great passion of the Christian's heart—to press forward unto what the apostle Paul called "perfection."

There were many things about the crucified life that interested Tozer. It was a life that was absolutely and irreconcilably incompatible with the world. It breathed the rarefied air of heaven while walking on earth. To the believer, it meant the absolute death of ego and the resurgence of Christ in his or her life. Emphatically, Tozer taught that Christ did not die on the cross just to save people from hell; rather, He died on the cross so that all could become one with Christ. That concept was so personally important to Tozer that anything that came between him and that unity with Christ had to be courageously dealt with and done away with, regardless of the cost.

The message of the crucified life was not a new concept. Tozer himself noted that all of the great Christians of the past wrote about this idea in some fashion. It was the unifying factor among a wide diversity of Christians down through the ages. The legacy of the church fathers, of the reformers, the re-vivalists, the Christian mystics and the hymnists all resonated on this one message. And while they might disagree on many points, in this one area there was a unique unity among them. The emphasis of the crucified life was to press forward—regard-less of the difficulties and in spite of the cost—to the state of spiritual perfection.

A Difficult Message

Tozer often confessed he would have preferred to simply talk about God all the time—about how wonderful God is and how wonderful it is to be on our way to heaven, enjoying the bless-ings of the Lord day by day. He would have preferred to preach such positive sermons. But the Spirit stirred him to keep press-ing the deep things of God. There was more to the Christian life than just being saved from the past and from one's sins. There was more to the Christian life than having a happy time on one's way to heaven.

Tozer saw the evangelical and fundamentalist churches of his day selling out to the world, just as the liberal churches did before them, and it disturbed him greatly. It bothered him to see these churches compromising with worldly values and slip-ping into the murky error of liberalism. It goaded him that the gospel churches were adopting worldly measures to build up church attendance, and he saw that many church leaders were using these things to promote themselves.

It was an era of what many called "easy believism." Simply put, the idea was that if you said you believed in Jesus, every-thing else would be all right. You did not have to change any-thing, for God loved you just the way you were. This kind of message stirred Dr. Tozer greatly. And Tozer was at his best when he was stirred.

It was for this reason that during the last years of his life, Tozer preached and wrote about the importance of living the crucified life. He felt an inward spiritual urging to sound the clarion call for the Church to return to the roots of the Christian message—the message of "Christ in you, the hope of glory" (Col. 1:27). Several times he said, "God did not call me to be a back scratcher," and anyone who heard him preach or read any of his editorials knew that was quite true. He was not interested in making people feel good about themselves; in fact, his agenda was quite the opposite. To Tozer, there was nothing good in man or even in the Christian—the only good was in Christ.

Tozer's goal was not to make attacks against a person, but he always sought to speak the truth as he saw it in love. As you might imagine, this did not always make him friends. One time, he told Dr. D. Martyn Lloyd-Jones of London that he had preached himself off every Bible conference in America. Of course, that was a bit exaggerated, because he was in demand at Bible conferences all across the country up until the time of his death. But some places did not invite him back. Regardless, he was tough and uncompromising on this issue because of what he felt was the seriousness of the condition of the evangelical church. He did not feel called of God to smooth ruffled feathers; rather, his calling was to ruffle some of those feathers.

Reverend Ray McAfee, a longtime associate pastor with Dr. A. W. Tozer, once told me the following story: Tozer was attending a holiness convention that was celebrating its fiftieth anniversary. He was the keynote speaker, and there were a number of preliminaries before he came to the pulpit. People were going around cutting other people's ties in half, there was impromptu singing along the lines of what we would call karaoke, and everybody was having a good old time celebrating the anniversary. McAfee could see Tozer tapping his right foot. The longer he sat there, the more he tapped his right foot. McAfee knew that Tozer was getting stirred.

When Tozer walked up to the pulpit, his first words were, "What's happened to you holiness people?" Then Tozer took them to the spiritual woodshed as they had never been taken before. Nothing was more serious to Tozer than the things of God. He had a sense of humor, but he did not consider the gathering of God's people to be a frivolous occasion but rather a time for worship and adoration of God. To Tozer, if you needed entertainment to get a crowd, it was not Christian.

The Challenge of the Crucified Life

This book is strong medicine for what Tozer considered a serious spiritual malady. The more serious the condition, the more radical the remedy; and for this reason, Tozer was willing to uncompromisingly confront people with the message of the crucified life.

It must be said that this message did not come without cost for Tozer. His friends and family often misunderstood him. He once wrote an editorial titled "The Saint Walks Alone," which he wrote from experience. It is easy to go along with the crowd, but the one who is committed to living the crucified life will always lean hard into the wind of opposition and misunderstanding.

Thus, living the crucified life is not an easy proposition—in fact, it will be the most challenging thing you will ever face. The cost is certainly high. The pathway is rough. The way forward is often lonely. But the rewards you will gain of knowing God in intimate fellowship will be well worth the journey.

Rev. James L. Snyder

PART I

THE
FOUNDATION
OF THE
CRUCIFIED
LIFE

1

THE IMPORTANCE OF THE CRUCIFIED LIFE

Knowing this, that our old man is crucified with him, that the body of sin might be destroyed, that henceforth we should not serve sin.

ROMANS 6:6

Nothing weighs heavier on my heart than the subject of this study. If it were not such a crucial Bible teaching, one could ignore the controversies and go on to something else. However, such is not the case. The subject of the crucified life is vitally important to the health and growth of the Church.

The Church is not some impersonal abstract floating around in space. Rather, the Church is comprised of individuals who have trusted Jesus Christ as their Lord and Savior. The health of the Church is in direct proportion to the health of each individual Christian. If the Church is to grow and be healthy, the individual Christians comprising the Church must grow spiritually. Only a dynamically healthy Church can ever hope to fulfill the commission of Christ to "go ye into all the world, and preach the gospel" (Mark 16:15).

One important thing needs to be understood. Not all Christians are alike. Jesus said in Matthew 13:23:

But he that received seed into the good ground is he that heareth the word, and understandeth it; which also beareth fruit, and bringeth forth, some an hundredfold, some sixty, some thirty.

Too many of us are satisfied to be thirtyfold Christians. But the desire of our Lord is that we press on to become hundredfold Christians. The question then is, how are we to go on to this stage?

This is the focus of this book. I think it my duty to prod the thirtyfold and the sixtyfold Christians to press on to the ultimate Christian experience, being a hundredfold Christian. The path that accomplishes this is living the crucified life. I do not think it would be amiss to say that most Christian literature today is focused on the thirtyfold Christians. Some might venture out and address the sixtyfold Christians, but it is safe to say there are few who focus on hundredfold Christians. This book is dedicated to that very thing. I simply call it *The Crucified Life*.

With that being the case, it is incumbent upon me to define some elements I will use throughout this study. If I use one term and the reader understands it in a different way from the manner in which I am using it, then communication breaks down. So let me define some of the basic concepts that will be developed throughout this study.

The Crucified Life

I first need to establish what I mean when I use the phrase "the crucified life." A variety of phrases have been used since apostolic days to define the subject—phrases such as "the deeper life," "the higher life," "the wholly sanctified life," "the spirit-filled life," "the victorious Christian life," "the exchanged life." But after looking at some of the literature produced on this topic, none seems to be any deeper, higher, holier or more Spirit-filled than common run-of-the-mill Christianity. For some, the phrase seems to be merely a catchphrase.

Strange Inconsistency

What I mean by "the crucified life" is a life wholly given over to the Lord in absolute humility and obedience: a sacrifice pleasing to the Lord. The word "crucified" takes us back to what Christ did on the cross. The key verse for this is Galatians 2:20:

> I am crucified with Christ: nevertheless I live; yet not I, but Christ liveth in me: and the life which I now live in the flesh I live by the faith of the Son of God, who loved me, and gave himself for me.

From the natural standpoint, the crucified life is burdened with contradictions. The biggest contradiction, of course, is the phrase itself: "crucified life." If a life is truly crucified, it is dead and not alive. But how can a person be dead and alive at the same time? Being dead and yet alive is one of the strange inconsistencies of the life established for us by Jesus' dying on the cross. But oh, the blessedness of these seeming inconsistencies.

Scriptural Proof

This study does not advocate any kind of Christian experience not based squarely on the plain teachings of the Scripture. Everything taught in this study must square with the entire Word of God. Anybody can prove anything by piecing together isolated texts. What is the teaching of the entire Word of God? That is the question that must be considered. Too much of contemporary Christianity is borrowed from the philosophies of the world and even other religions—phrases and mottos that on the surface look great but are not rooted in Scripture or that mostly bolster one's self-image.

Whatever the teaching might be or whoever the teacher might be, we must strongly demand scriptural proof. If such proof cannot be presented, then the teaching must be rejected out of mind and out of hand. This may sound legalistic, but it is one of the absolutes that is part of the Christian experience. The Christian lives and dies by the Book.

I am not advocating in this study anything that cannot be proved by Scripture, and I do not mean just a verse here and there, but by the whole counsel of God. We believe in the whole Bible, not bits and pieces. The whole Bible supports the idea of progressing toward spiritual perfection in our Christian lives. Spiritual perfection is what the apostle Paul longed for and spoke about:

> Not as though I had already attained, either were already perfect: but I follow after, if that I may apprehend that for which also I am apprehended of Christ Jesus (Phil. 3:12).

The crucified life is a life absolutely committed to following after Christ Jesus. To be more like Him. To think like Him. To act like Him. To love like Him. The whole essence of spiritual perfection has everything to do with Jesus Christ. Not with rules and regulations. Not with how we dress or what we do or do not do. We are not to look like each other; rather, we are to look like Christ. We can get all caught up in the nuances of religion and miss the glorious joy of following after Christ. Whatever hinders us in our journey must be dealt a deathblow.

The Christian Mystics

Throughout this study will be quotes from some of the great Christian mystics going back to the days of the apostles. It is important to define what I mean by "mystic." This term has been much abused in the house of its friends. Perhaps it would be good to use another term for this, but every time something is renamed, it loses some of its original meaning. Therefore, without any regret or hesitation, I will stick with this old term.

I have found throughout my study that these old saints of God, the mystics, really knew God. "Mystic," then, refers to someone who has an intimate, a direct, relationship with God. In my pursuit of God, I want to know what they knew of God and how they came to know Him on such intimate grounds. (This is not to say I agree with everything they wrote, as I would not agree with everything anybody else would write.)

Back on the farm in Pennsylvania, we had an old apple tree. It was a gnarly, stark-looking tree. A casual glance at this tree might tempt a person to pass it up. Regardless of how terrible the tree looked, however, it produced some of the most delicious apples I have ever eaten. I endured the gnarly branches in order to enjoy the delicious fruit.

I feel the same way about some of these grand old mystics of the Church. They may look gnarly and austere, but they produced wonderful spiritual fruit. The fruit is what really matters, not the appearance. It matters not if the man wears a robe or a suit; it is the man that really counts. I am willing to overlook a lot if the writer genuinely knows God and "knows God other than by hearsay," as Thomas Carlyle used to say. Too many only repeat what they have heard from somebody who heard it from somebody else. It is refreshing to hear an original voice. Each of these mystics had that original voice.

The Church has always had this group of people—both men and women—who had such a hunger for God and a passion to know Him that everything else took second place. Many of them were harassed and tormented by the established Church.

Some even were martyred because of this uncontrollable passion for God. Many of them lived prior to the Reformation and had no idea what a protestant or even an evangelical was. For the most part, they were not interested in labels. They were only interested in pursuing God.

These men and women were not protestant, Catholic, fundamentalist or evangelical; they were simply Christians in hot pursuit of God. They had no banner to wave except Jehovah-Nissi. They had no honor to preserve apart from Jesus Christ. They gave witness to a life ablaze with love and adoration for God that nothing can extinguish. Not all the years since their death have been able to quench the fervor of their love for God.

Fortunately, for us, some of the great devotional literature of the Church that these men and women gave their lives to write has been preserved. In reading these great works, one is transported out of time and into the mystical wonder of pursuing God. It is as if time has no bearing between the author and the reader. It is hard to read such material for long without feeling the heartbeat of the author's passion. This, in my opinion, is what is missing among Christians today, especially in the evangelical church.

Pick up any hymnal, particularly an old one, and you will find many hymns by these great Christian mystics. Their pursuit of God is only matched by their desire to share the object of their love with any and all who will listen. Perhaps one of their quotes throughout this study will light a fire in your heart.

The *King James Version* Bible

To avoid confusion, I need to mention why I use the *King James Version* throughout this study. Although I have every Bible translation imaginable, I still place the *King James Version* at the top of the list of my Bibles to read. I certainly am not against other translations. In fact, I am usually the first one to buy the newest translation, but I give predominance to this version in my reading and study.

I know all the arguments against the *King James Version*, but answer me this: If it is as bad as some scholars tell us, why has God blessed it so much? More people have come into the kingdom of God through this blessed translation than any other. It has been translated into more languages than any other version; perhaps more than all the rest put together.

Does it not seem strange that the generation with the most advanced technology and the easiest-to-read Bible translations is the weakest generation of Christians in the history of our country? Church attendance has never been lower, and the Christian influence in our culture never weaker.

For so long we have heard the complaint that people do not read and study the Bible because the language is antiquated. Yet the generation who had only the *King James Version* was the generation that sparked revivals and missionary movements around the world. It just may be that the Bible translation was not the problem. It is my observation that the natural man does not understand spiritual principles. The problem has never been the translation. The problem has never been academic. The problem has always been spiritual.

One important point many fail to understand is that the Bible was never meant to replace God; rather, it was meant to lead us into the heart of God. Too many Christians stop with the text and never go on to experience the presence of God.

The "old" *King James Version* has been so mightily used of God that it deserves a place of honor in our reading and study. Even the most casual reflection on the past will reveal that the Spirit of God has used it to move upon men, opening up their hearts and minds to understand the Scriptures. It has always been "the Spirit itself beareth witness with our spirit, that we are the children of God" (Rom. 8:16).

I would recommend that you go to some secondhand bookstore and buy a used *King James* Bible. You might have to put down a few dollars, but it will be the best investment you have ever made. I know the "thees" and "thous" are rather cumbersome, but one of the most beautiful things about these words is that they slow you down when you read. Probably there is no greater offense in all of Christendom than speed-reading the Bible. The Bible must be read slowly and meditatively, allowing the Spirit of God to open up our understanding.

The Christian Hymnal

The last thing I want to define is "the Christian hymnal." My heart aches as I see this increasingly being neglected by congregations. The Christian hymnal is one of the great depositories of the Christian life and experience. The men and women behind these hymns were writing out of deep spiritual experiences. The poetry of some hymns may not be perfect. In fact, some may be very difficult to sing. Pushing the hymnal aside, however, is to forfeit one of the great spiritual treasures of the Christian Church. The hymnal connects us with our Christian heritage, a legacy that should not be denied to this generation of Christians. If we are going to press on to be hundredfold Christians, on to Christian perfection and the crucified life, we need this vital connection to the historic Church.

Show me the condition of your Bible and your hymnal and I will accurately predict the condition of your soul. Our souls need to be nurtured and cultivated, and nothing does that better than the Christian hymnal. I cannot imagine a Christian not spending quality time in the hymnal. Hardly a morning passes when I don't kneel down with an open Bible and a hymnal and sing comfortably off-key the great hymns of the Church.

I often counsel young Christians, after they have their Bible and their Bible reading established, to get a hymnal. If a young Christian would spend one year reading through and meditating on the hymns of Isaac Watts alone, he would have a better theological education than four years in Bible college and four years in seminary. Isaac Watts and others like him were able to put theology into their hymns. These hymn writers—both men and women—set their generation singing theology. And the theology of the heart bursts forth in melodious adoration and praise.

Pursuing the Crucified Life

Living the crucified life is a journey not for the faint at heart. The journey is rough and filled with dangers and difficulties, and it does not end until we see Christ. Yet though the journey may be difficult, the result of seeing Christ face to face is worth it all.

Face to Face
Carrie E. Breck (1855–1934)

Face to face with Christ my Savior,
Face to face—what will it be,
When with rapture I behold Him,
Jesus Christ, who died for me?

Face to face I shall behold Him,
Far beyond the starry sky;
Face to face in all His glory,
I shall see Him by and by!

Only faintly now I see Him,
With the darkened veil between;
But a blessed day is coming,
When His glory shall be seen.

What rejoicing in His presence,
When are banished grief and pain;
When the crooked ways are straightened,
And the dark things shall be plain!

Face to face! O blissful moment!
Face to face to see and know;
Face to face with my Redeemer,
Jesus Christ, who loves me so.

2

THE FOUNDATION OF THE CHRISTIAN EXPERIENCE

*God, who at sundry times and in divers manners spake in time past
unto the fathers by the prophets, hath in these last days spoken
unto us by his Son, whom he hath appointed heir of all things,
by whom also he made the worlds.*

HEBREWS 1:1-2

An old Chinese proverb says the journey of 1,000 miles begins
with the first step. If that first step is not taken, nothing else
really matters. If you are not on the journey, talking about it
does not matter. Many Christians talk about living the crucified life but nothing in their lives indicates they have even begun the journey.

Among the thirtyfold Christians, there is much joy that
they have been saved but no anticipation of continuing on the
journey toward spiritual perfection. They are so happy they
are not what they used to be that they cannot see what God
wants them to be.

Christianity has a glorious and victorious side that few
Christians experience. If I have anything to say to the Church
of Christ and evangelicals in the world, it is in this area of the
victorious Christian life, this living the crucified life.

Our weakness is that we are not going on to know Christ in enriched intimacy and acquaintance; and, worse, we are not even talking about it. We rarely hear about it, and it does not get into our magazines, our books or any kind of media ministry and it is not found in our churches. What I am talking about is this yearning, this longing to know God in increasing measure. This yearning should push us forward to spiritual perfection.

I believe two basic reasons explain this. One has to do with Bible teaching on the deeper Christian experience: Most churches never get beyond the basic teaching of becoming a Christian. Even then, the teaching is quite watered-down and usually focuses on the fact that someday we are going to die and go to heaven. The other reason has to do with the cost. Many are not willing to pay the cost associated with the victorious Christian life. Erroneously, many are taught and believe that the Christian life is a free ride that eventually ends in heaven. After all, Jesus paid it all.

Throughout this study, I want to address these two factors.

What Is a Christian?

The first factor to address is simply, what is a Christian?

All kinds of definitions are floating around, but only those rooted in Scripture are valid. How many people think they are Christians because someone told them they were? Imagine going through life believing you are a Christian because someone told you that you were; then you die and find out you were not.

Quite simply put, a Christian is one who sustains a right relationship with Jesus Christ. A Christian enjoys a kind of union with Jesus Christ superseding all other relationships.

This is the generation of questions. Everybody seems to have his own question. Questions are important to ask, but it is more important to ask the right ones. A successful lawyer will win or lose a case simply by the questions he asks or does not ask. There is no end to questions, and we can be bogged down trying to answer each and every little one. Finding our way through the maze of questions today is an all-but-impossible ride.

I believe this whole thing can be boiled down to one important question that, if answered correctly, will solve all the other questions and make them irrelevant.

The Important Question

It was never in the mind of Peter to talk about the heroic example of our Lord. Christ's teachings were noble, and His example is well worth imitating. The New Testament centers the emphasis on Christ crucified and risen and presents Him as the last alternate object of faith. The important question to ask, then, is not just "what is a Christian?" but "what think ye of Christ?"

Today's evangelical church is abuzz with questions. A person can spend all his time trying to answer them. "What do you think of the Bible?" "What do you think of the Church?" And there are others we could note, but all these questions are completely out of date.

For example, the question, "What do you think of the Bible?" is outdated and has no meaning since the Bible was confirmed by the resurrection of Jesus Christ. Jesus Christ endorsed the Bible in its entirety.

The question, "What do you think of the Church?" has no meaning either. Nobody can ask that and be truly sincere about it because Christ said, "On this rock I will build my church and the gates of hell shall not prevail against it" (Matt. 18:18).

These questions, and many more like them, are inappropriate. So the question before us, and the question that really matters, is simply, what do you think of Christ? And what are you going to do with Christ? Every question we might ever have can be boiled down to the subject of Jesus Christ.

Everybody needs to answer this question of what we are going to do about this man whom God raised from the dead. Christ is the last word of God to humankind. It is written:

> God, who at sundry times and in divers manners spake in time past unto the fathers by the prophets, hath in these last days spoken unto us by his Son, whom he hath appointed heir of all things, by whom also he made the worlds (Heb. 1:1-2).

It is also written that "the Word was made flesh, and dwelt among us" (John 1:14). When the Word became flesh, God spoke. He spoke His Word in flesh, and the incarnated Christ is that Word. That sums up all that God would ever say to men. No new development in human psychology requires God to amend or edit what He has already said in Jesus Christ.

Our question then is about Christ Himself, and all other religious questions are reduced to, "what do you think of Christ and what are you going to do about Him?" Unless this is fully addressed, nothing else really matters.

Some pretend to have problems concerning this. Actually, they are in love with themselves and are blinded by egotism and self-love. I respectfully claim the right to doubt the sanity of those who are now saying, "I have problems about the Bible. I have problems about the Church. I have problems about morality." All these problems are reduced to one. God spake His eternal Word in Christ Jesus the Lord, so Christ has settled every question.

The question of honest seekers looking for proof of Christianity is bogus. God's raising His Son from the dead is the only proof, and that proof is infinitely capable of settling the mind of anyone who is concerned and who is sincere. So the question is not what proof is there of Christianity, because we are not dealing with Christianity. We are dealing with Christ. We are dealing with a man who became flesh, walked among men, gave His life for man and, to complete it, rose on the third day from the dead. The question is not what you think of Christianity but what you think of Christ and what you are going to do about Him.

Neither does the sincere man ask, "Is Christ who and what He claimed to be?" Some claim they have doubts and question whether Christ is who and what He claimed about Himself. There should be no question here at all, because the Scripture says Jesus was approved of God among men (see Acts 2:22). Great volumes of books have been written that would fill any building from the cellar to the roof trying to show that Jesus is what He claimed to be. The worshiping heart knows He is what He claimed to be because God sent the Holy Spirit to carry the confirmation to the conscience of man. It does not lie with evidence. History can offer no higher evidence than the fact that God raised Christ from the dead and set Him at His own right hand.

Jesus' Moral Teachings

The question of the sincere man is not, "How does Jesus compare with the teachings of the moral philosophers and the religions of the world?" Some present this question with an air of pretentious self-importance. This question is settled forever because the moral teachings of Jesus stand or fall with Him. Let any man take issue with Christ and he is done as far as being a Christian is concerned. No one can take issue with the Lord; no one can question the truth of the Truthful One; no one dare bring up the matter of whether or not Jesus is the Lord or whether His teachings are sound or whether He is approved of God. His moral teachings stand or fall with Him. Jesus Christ our Lord Himself is the object of our attention, not the teachings of Jesus.

The teachings of Jesus are dear to us, and through them it is possible to keep His commandments and prove we love Him. It is the person of Jesus that makes His teachings valid. God put the proof down on a spiritual level. It does not rest on reason but on conscience. If the resurrection of Christ were to rest on reason, then only the highly reasonable people could be converted. If the resurrection of Christ were to rest on man's ability to gather and weigh evidence, then the man trained in the gathering and evaluating of evidence might believe, but the simple-hearted man could never believe. The man who works with his hands and does not do much deep thinking would remain unconverted. With Christ it was just the opposite. The common people heard Him gladly.

A "Pricked" Heart

The appeal of Jesus Christ was always to the simple-hearted man who was troubled by his conscience. He brought a troubled and lacerated conscience to Christ. The conscience knew that Christ had risen and appeared to Peter and 500 brethren at once, and God had approved Him, confirmed Him, validated Him, marked Him, sealed Him and proved Him to be His Christ.

All kinds of people are converted, and not because they have the ability to weigh evidence. If salvation depended on my ability to know if a thing were true or not, or on my ability to know as a court of law whether it witnesses to the truth or not, then of course only lawyers and persons trained in the legal profession would have any possibility of salvation. But this truth of Christ rising from the dead leaps past all human reason, rises above it and goes straight to the conscience of every person so that as soon as a message is preached, everybody can know it immediately. They do not have to ask. They do not need to ask. In fact, it is an affront to ask. Jesus Christ is risen and has appeared to His disciples. God confirmed His resurrection, sent down the Holy Spirit, and now the Most High God Himself, maker of heaven and earth, has already rendered the verdict. God has sent His Spirit to carry the verdict to the conscience of man.

According to the testimony in Acts 2:37, the result of Peter's preaching was that men "were pricked in their hearts." The word "pricked" here simply means pierced lightly. Pierced lightly and yet so deep that the original Greek word had a qualifying and intensifying prefix on it. When the Scripture says they pierced the side of Jesus with the spear and found that He was already dead (see John 19:34), the word "pierced" is translated from one word. The original word used in Acts has a qualifying and intensifying prefix to it, indicating that the words of Peter went further into the hearts of the hearers then the spear of the soldier went into the side of Jesus. So the Holy Spirit carried the spear point of truth into the hearts of the people and they cried, "What shall we do?" (Acts 2:37). Peter had the answer for them immediately:

> Repent, and be baptized every one of you in the name of Jesus Christ for the remission of sins, and ye shall receive the gift of the Holy Ghost.

Peter was saying, "You are to believe on the Lord Jesus Christ and then prove you believed by identifying yourself with Him in baptism. You are to identify yourself with Him in baptism and prove and show to the world that you believe in this One that has been raised from the dead." The people gladly received his word and were baptized, and that same day about 3,000 were added to the Church (see Acts 2:41). Facts and reason cannot have such an effect. I could argue with a man, I could reason with him, I could preach to him, and if I were capable of doing so with the oratory of Cicero or Demosthenes, when it was all over I could only convince his mind.

Our consciences can be awakened by the presence of Jesus having come out of the grave. Some people have been fooled into believing that it was the life of Jesus that saved us. No, He had to die. Some say it was at the death of Jesus that we were saved. No, He had to rise from the dead. All three acts had to be present before we could truly say we have a Savior we can trust. He had to live among men, holy and harmless, spotless and undefiled. He had to die for man and then rise on the third day, according to the Scripture. He did all three. What the Spirit of God carries back home to the heart the Holy Spirit impales on our consciences, and we cannot escape until we have done something about Jesus.

What Is the Cost?

The second factor to address is what is the cost of the crucified life. Yes, Jesus paid for our salvation, but there still is a cost we must each pay. The Christian life is not a free ride.

The "Do" Condition

What shall we do? Peter was never afraid of the word "do." Some in evangelical circles are afraid of the word "do." They all but infer that it is an improper word. But Peter was not afraid of that at all, because it is not the "do" of merit—it is the "do" of condition. What should I do that I may receive the benefits of the Lord Jesus Christ into my life? Peter said, "Believe on the Lord Jesus Christ and identify yourself with Him by baptism."

That is what we are supposed to do. That is what Easter means, and you cannot escape it. We may only celebrate it once a year, but it haunts us all year; and if in the providence of God you should die this year, it will haunt you to the grave and throughout eternity. For God has given His Son, Jesus Christ, to the world and said, "Believe on my Son":

Whosoever believeth in him shall not perish . . . [and whosoever] believeth not is condemned already, because he hath not believed in the name of the only begotten son of God (John 3:16-18).

This is the "do" of condition. If Christ is alive, then you must *do* something about Him. If He is alive, then He is on your conscience until you have done something about it. And that He is alive is proven by the coming down of the Holy Ghost to carry the evidence straight to the conscience of man.

An Impaled Conscience

Thank God, He lives. Thank God, the fight is over. Thank God, the battle is won and the victory of life is ours. But until you have done something about it, it is on your conscience and will remain there until the ages have rolled away. He is on the conscience of millions who are doing nothing about it and trying to live a crucified life without facing it.

Others may try to do that, but I cannot. Christ died for me. He took my sins. God raised Him from the dead and sent the Holy Spirit to say, "This is my beloved Son . . . hear ye him" (Matt. 17:5).

So I must hear, I must listen, I must identify, I must admit, I must follow, I must devote, I must dedicate. I must follow the Lamb wherever He goes. He is on my conscience until I do. My conscience is impaled with the fact that He rose again in triumph of the resurrection and the confirmation of the saving grace for the whole human race.

Christianity rests upon one foundation: Jesus Christ. Before anyone can understand the depth of Christian experience and the dynamics of living the crucified life, this foundation needs to be established. No building can ever exceed the capacity of its foundation. The more important the building, the more important the foundation.

The right question to ask is simply, "who is Jesus Christ?" And closely following that is, "what am I going to do with Him?"

What Will You Do with Jesus?
A. B. Simpson (1843–1919)

Jesus is standing in Pilate's hall,
Friendless, forsaken, betrayed by all;
Hearken! what meaneth the sudden call?
What will you do with Jesus?

What will you do with Jesus?
Neutral you cannot be;
Some day your heart will be asking,
"What will He do with me?"

Jesus is standing on trial still,
You can be false to Him if you will,
You can be faithful through good or ill:
What will you do with Jesus?

Will you evade him as Pilate tried?
Or will you choose Him, whate'er betide?

Vainly you struggle from Him to hide:
What will you do with Jesus?

Will you, like Peter, your Lord deny?
Or will you scorn from His foes to fly,
Daring for Jesus to live or die?
What will you do with Jesus?

"Jesus, I give Thee my heart today!
Jesus, I'll follow Thee all the way,
Gladly obeying Thee!" will you say:
"This I will do with Jesus!"

3

THE RESURRECTION SIDE OF THE CROSS

If ye then be risen with Christ, seek those things which are above, where Christ sitteth on the right hand of God. Set your affection on things above, not on things on the earth. For ye are dead, and your life is hid with Christ in God.

COLOSSIANS 3:1-3

The starting point of our journey is knowing who Jesus Christ really is. It is at this point we set our faith like a flint toward the heavenly Jerusalem. Our ultimate goal is to see Christ face to face. As with every other type of journey, so the journey of living the crucified life has many obstacles. If we rest upon our own strength, we fail. However, there is strength in Jesus Christ that makes the Christian journey successful.

Success in the Christian life is not automatic. The soul must be cultivated like a garden and the will must be sanctified and become Christian through and through. Heavenly treasures must be sought, and we must seek those things that are above and mortify the things that are below. This may not be written about much in the annals of the modern evangelical church, but it *is* written in the New Testament.

Too many are satisfied with the status quo and never press on to become hundredfold Christians. Satisfied with just "being," many do not go on to "doing." Our objective is to finish the race. Many begin, but few cross the finish line. What is the secret to pressing on? Where is the strength to be found to endure the race until the very end?

The Reason for Everything

Christ's triumph over death, the foundation and fountain of our faith, was everything to the early enraptured believers. Christ's rising from the dead was first an amazing thing, then it became a joyful wonder, and then a radiance of conviction supported by many infallible proofs, witnessed to by the Holy Ghost. This became to the first Christians the reason for everything.

The battle cry of those early Christians was "He is risen," and it became to them outright courage. In the first 200 years, hundreds of thousands of Christians died as martyrs. To those early Christians, Easter was not a holiday or even a holy day. It was not a day at all. It was an accomplished fact that lived with them all year long and became the reason for their daily conduct. "He lives," they said, "and we live. He was triumphant, and in Him we are triumphant. He is with us and leads us and we follow."

They turned their faces toward an altogether new life because Christ was raised from the dead. They did not celebrate His rising from the dead and then go back to their everyday lives and wait for another year to pull them up from out of the mire. They *lived* by the fact that Christ had risen from the dead and they had risen with Him.

"If ye then be risen with Christ . . ." That word "if" is not an "if" of uncertainty. The force of the word is "since ye are then risen with Christ." Paul declared in Romans 6:4, Ephesians 2:6-7 and elsewhere that when Christ rose from the dead, His people rose with Him. Mortality rose with Him. Spirituality rose with Him. And this rising from the dead was and is an accomplished fact.

The Treasures of Heaven

What does Paul mean when he talks about "those things which are above"? This is not some broad generalization as it may sound. They can be identified. We may draw a line down the middle of a page and over on the left-hand side put the things that are of the earth, and over on the right-hand side the things that are of heaven. The things that are of earth belong to sight, reason and our senses. The things that are in heaven belong to faith, trust and confidence in God.

Over on the left-hand side, we put pleasures of the earth, and over on the right-hand side, we put delight in the Lord. On the left we put treasures of the earth; on the right we put treasures "where neither moth nor rust doth corrupt, and where thieves do not break through nor steal" (Matt. 6:20). On the left, we put reputation among men and our desire to stand well with men; on the right we put our desire to stand high with God. Over on the left we put a rich dwelling place; over on the right we put a mansion above. On the left, we put a desire to walk with the best company here below; on the right we put a desire to walk with God here below. On the left, we put following man's philosophy, and on the right, following God's revelations. On the left, cultivating the flesh; on the right, living for the Spirit. On the left, to live for a time; on the right, to live for eternity.

By contrast, we see how different we are as Christians. We are to be so different from the world, so completely different. Go down the left-hand side and you will have sight, reason and senses; they give you the pleasures of the earth that make you want the treasures of the earth. They want you to want a good reputation among men and a rich dwelling place here. They make you want to walk with the best company and follow man's philosophy.

The things that are of God make our faith, trust and confidence in God and make us delight in the Lord and value the treasures that are above. They want us to stand high with God in a mansion in heaven, to walk with God below and follow God's revelation, and to live for the soul and for eternity.

A Church Different from the World

Paul writes to Christians to address a great mistake that we are always making. We must know better, but we are always confusing the world with the Church and trying to get the world to do what we have difficulty getting Christians to do. We are always preaching sermons, writing articles and singing hymns trying to equate our country and our modern civilization—or any civilization—with Christianity. It cannot be done.

The Christian Church is something apart. It is not black or white or red or yellow. The Christian Church is not for Canadians or Americans or Germans or British or Japanese. The Christian Church is a new creation born of the Holy Ghost out of the stuff of Christ's wounded side, and it is another race altogether. It is a people, or a race, held above this present race, and we are to be different from the world because we are risen with Christ. "Seek those things that are above and set your will—set your mind—on the things that are above where Christ sits on the right hand of God." That is the heart and truth.

The Scriptures teach us that Christ is out of the grave, alive for evermore and constantly present for those who have faith. He gathers with His people wherever they meet, anytime they meet—even in a cave, hiding from persecution. It may be a mule barn or it may be a cathedral, but wherever the people of God gather, there is God in the midst of them. They minister to the Lord and pray. So the Church of Christ lives because Christ lives, and it does not depend on seasons of the year. Christ is out of the grave and will never be back in that grave again. Death has no more dominion over Him. Therefore, because He is risen from the grave, we too are to be risen with Him and to seek those things that are above.

Certain imperatives are set before us because Christ is risen, and every holy voice from heaven above cries and exhorts that we should perform these commands and live with them. The Scriptures say "seek" and "set." "Seek . . . and set your affections on things above" and put off the old ways, forgive everybody in the world and dedicate your time to Him.

Too often, we give God only the tired remnants of our time. If Jesus Christ had given us only the remnant of His time, we would all be on our way to that darkness that knows no morning. Christ gave us not the tattered leftovers of His time; He gave us all the time He had. But some of us give Him only the leftovers of our money and of our talents and never give our time fully to the Lord Jesus Christ who gave us all. Because He gave all, we have what we have; and He calls us "as he is, so are we in this world" (1 John 4:17).

Cultivation of a Religious Mind

As an example, we ought to have Christian minds. Our difficulty is that we have a secular mind and a religious mind. With the secular mind, we do most everything that we do, and then we have a little private party for what we call the religious minds. With our religious mind we try to serve the Lord the best we can. It does not work that way. The Christian should not have any secular mind at all. If you are a Christian, you should "seek the things that are above"—there should be no worldly mind in you.

Some might ask, "How can I pursue my studies? How can I do my housework? How can I carry on my business?" You carry on your business, do your housework and pursue your studies by making them a part of an offering to God as certainly as the money you put in the offering plate or anything else you give openly and publicly to God.

Living the crucified life precludes this divided life. A life that is partly secular, partly spiritual, partly of this world and partly of the world above is not what the New Testament teaches at all. As Christians, we can turn some of the most hopeless jobs into wonderful spiritual prayer meetings, if we will simply turn them over to God.

Nicolas Herman, who was commonly known as Brother Lawrence, was a simple dishwasher in the institution where he lived. He said he did those dishes for the glory of God. When he was through with his humble work, he would fall down flat on the floor and worship God. Whatever he was told to do, he did it for the glory of God. He testified, "I wouldn't as much as pick up a straw from the floor, but I did it for the glory of God."

One saint praised God every time he drank a glass of water. He did not make a production out of it, but in his heart, he thanked God. Every time I leave my house, I look to God, expecting Him to bless me and keep me on my way. Every time I am flying in the air, I expect Him to keep me there, land me safely and bring me back. If He wants me in heaven more than He wants me on earth, then He will answer no to that prayer and it will be all over—but I will be with Him over there. In the meantime, while He wants me here, I will thank Him every hour and every day for everything.

Let us do away with our secular and worldly minds and cultivate sanctified minds. We have to do worldly jobs, but if we do them with sanctified minds, they no longer are worldly but are as much a part of our offering to God as anything else we give to Him.

Behavior Like an Awkward Goose

Christ is risen, and we have risen with Him and sit at the right hand of the Father with Him in spirit—and one of these days with a human body. In the meantime, we're to act as if we are up there in heaven, but a little bit different. A farm boy comes to the city and acts different because he belongs on the farm. The city boy goes to the country and acts different because he belongs in the city. The man who has not been on a farm walks around gingerly, trying to keep out of the mud and keep his shoes from being soiled. He is acting like a city man on the farm. As Christians, we ought to act that way.

In a manner of speaking, we belong up there. Our culture belongs up there. Our thinking belongs up there. Everything belongs up there. Of course, when you are down here, people recognize you and say, "Well, that fellow belongs in heaven." I know a lot of people that belong in heaven. I suppose one of the ugliest things in all of the world is a goose walking around on the earth. But one of the most graceful sights in the skies is a wild goose with its wings spread on its way south or north. I suppose we act awkward here because we belong up there.

Those of you who work in big offices surrounded by people who are not Christians cannot easily fit into the conversation when break time comes. You act awkwardly, and you are worried and ashamed and wonder why. It is because you belong to God. You have another spirit; you know another language, and you speak this world's language with an accent.

When others mention religion, they talk about it with an accent. They belong to the earth; you belong to God in the skies and, of course, they do not agree. They think you walk awkwardly down here, but they have not seen you with your wings spread yet. Wait until the time comes when the children of God spread their wings and soar away to meet Him in glory. Then they will see how graceful they are. While on earth, of course, they do not think we are.

Jewels on This Earth

This matter of being hidden with Christ in God can be naturally divided quite into four segments. The first point, "your life." The second point, "is hid." The third point, "with Christ." Then the last point, "in God." Here are the jewels on the earth from the sky. Your faith is strengthened assurance, and here is the cure of all cures: "your life is hid with Christ in God."

The hope of the Church is that "when Christ, who is our life, shall appear, then shall ye also appear with him in glory" (Col. 3:4). That is the hope of the Church. Not all the details. We were too smart a generation ago when we thought we knew all the details. Everybody knew exactly everything that could be known about prophecy. It has gone the other way now. Everybody is afraid to talk about prophecy, because what we had been taught has been kicked out from under us and some of our views. No question, He will come and when He does come, you will be with Him in glory. Just as you were with Him when He died and with Him when He rose, you will be with Him when He comes in glory. In the meantime, you are supposed to act as you believe.

It's just like the new bride who must be separated for a little while from her bridegroom. She writes some letters and eagerly calls him long-distance. She wants to be with him. He is out there somewhere, trying to get a home together for them. She says, "I don't care about the house. I want to be with you." It is not the house with the trimmings and the furniture and all the rest that's important. She longs for *him*. So it is with Jesus Christ. We want Jesus Christ, and the glory will take care of itself.

The Glory of God

I have read the book of Revelation and the hymns of the church and have tried to learn what I can about the glory. Most of us do not know too much about heaven yet. We may be surprised by what we see there and what we call the glory. We cannot know any more than we do now until He comes, but we can know it with increasing intimacy. By knowing Him we will know the glory, because He *is* the glory of that place—the Lamb is the light there.

Living the crucified life begins on the resurrection side of the cross. Jesus is alive; therefore, we live. But it is not I. It is Christ all the way.

Christ the Lord Is Risen Today
Charles Wesley (1707–1788)

Christ the Lord is risen today, Alleluia!
Sons of men and angels say: Alleluia!
Raise your joys and triumphs high, Alleluia!
Sing, ye heavens, and earth reply: Alleluia!

Lives again our glorious King, Alleluia!
Where, O death, is now thy sting? Alleluia!
Dying once, He all doth save, Alleluia!
Where thy victory, O grave? Alleluia!

Love's redeeming work is done, Alleluia!
Fought the fight, the battle won, Alleluia!

Death in vain forbids Him rise, Alleluia!
Christ hath opened paradise, Alleluia!

Soar we now where Christ hath led, Alleluia!
Following our exalted Head, Alleluia!
Made like Him, like Him we rise, Alleluia!
Ours the cross, the grave, the skies, Alleluia!

Vain the stone, the watch, the seal, Alleluia!
Christ hath burst the gates of hell, Alleluia!
Death in vain forbids His rise, Alleluia!
Christ hath opened paradise, Alleluia!

4

THE LONELINESS OF THE CRUCIFIED LIFE

One thing have I desired of the LORD, that will I seek after;
that I may dwell in the house of the LORD all the days of my life,
to behold the beauty of the LORD, and to enquire in his temple.

PSALM 27:4

The man who wrote Psalm 27 was David. David sought after God because he knew that "they that seek the LORD shall not want any good thing" (Ps. 34:10). He said, "My soul thirsteth after thee, as a thirsty land" (Ps. 143:6). Further, David said, "Truly my soul waiteth upon God: from him cometh my salvation. . . . My soul, wait thou only upon God; for my expectation is from him" (Ps. 62:1-5). David also said, "O God, thou art my God; early will I seek thee: my soul thirsteth for thee, my flesh longeth for thee in a dry and thirsty land, where no water is" (Ps. 63:1). David continually says, "My soul followeth hard after thee: thy right hand doth upholdeth me" (Ps. 63:8).

That is the language of the man David. You will find this same tone going back to Abraham and reaching all the way through the Old Testament. Today we seek God and stop searching, whereas the early saints sought God, found Him and continued to seek more of Him.

Follow After and Love Deeply

Some great souls seem very unusual to us because of this tone in their lives. I do not set any of them on a pedestal, for they get their virtue where we get ours—from the Lord Jesus Christ. Their merit comes from the same fount as ours; and ours, the same as theirs. The apostle Paul said, "Not as though I had already attained, either were already perfect: but I follow after, if that I may apprehend that for which also I am apprehended of Christ Jesus" (Phil. 3:12).

This produced people like Saint Augustine and John Tauler, Thomas à Kempis, Richard Rolle, Bernard of Clairvaux, Bernard of Cluny, John of the Cross, Madame Guyon, François Fénelon and Henry Suso. These names may sound unfamiliar to some but they were associated with the "longing after" Christian crowd, those who cultivated the same tone in their hearts as David of old.

I could name names that might be more familiar: Samuel Rutherford, John Wesley, A. B. Simpson. A thirsting and a longing for the cool water *drove* these men and women. When they found Him, they sought Him again. What a tragedy it has been that in our time, we are taught to believe in Him and accept Him, and to seek Him no more.

This is where the evangelical church is today. What I am trying to do is encourage people to want to seek God. Any arrow toward the target must be going in the right direction. It is the direction and the motion that matters. If God is the direction and if you are moving toward God, then I am happy.

In the Old Testament is a book few people read. I hesitate to read it myself, because it is a little raw. Most people do not read it because they do not know what it means. I am referring to the Song of Solomon. One of the old mystics, Bernard of Clairvaux, started to write a series of sermons on the Song of Solomon (*Sermons on the Song of Songs*), but he had only finished preaching the first chapter at the time his death. So I suppose he finished it over in glory.

The Song of Solomon is the story of a girl deeply in love with a young shepherd. It is quite a wonderful love story indeed and has been understood so by the Church. One of Charles Wesley's hymns, "Thou Shepherd of Israel, and Mine," is based on this book:

Thou Shepherd of Israel, and mine,
The joy and desire of my heart,
For closer communion I pine,
I long to reside where thou art:
The pasture I languish to find
Where all, who their Shepherd obey,
Are fed, on thy bosom reclined,
And screened from the heat of the day.

Ah! show me that happiest place,
The place of thy people's abode,
Where saints in an ecstasy gaze,
And hang on a crucified God:
Thy love for a sinner declare,
Thy passion and death on the tree;
My spirit to Calvary bear,
To suffer and triumph with thee.

'Tis there, with the lambs of thy flock,
There only I covet to rest,
To lie at the foot of the rock,
Or rise to be hid in thy breast;
'Tis there I would always abide,
And never a moment depart,
Concealed in the cleft of thy side,
Eternally held in thy heart.

This great hymn talks about God without being flippant. Our mentality today, however, is an "I believe in Christ; now let's go have a soda" type of Christianity. The Church of Jesus Christ never runs on its head. The Church runs on its heart. The Holy Spirit never fills a man's head. The Holy Spirit fills his heart. The efforts today to "assist" Christianity with philosophy and science are going to get a cold frown from almighty God, and then He will let them go, little by little, their blind way into liberalism. Somewhere God will have Himself a people, and they will be those who continue to cry after Him whom they love.

This is no place for human ethics. The anonymous author of *The Cloud of Unknowing* wrote, "Of the shortness of this word, and how it may not be come to by curiosity of wit, nor by imagination. . . . Remember him by longing of God both tried to think their way through." In other words, it is not through your thinking or imagination that you will reach God. In all of this, there is an element of the unknown.

Futile Thinking

I will not settle for anything less than the deep divine addiction that we call God, and I will strive to live beyond the power of thought or visualization. The primary difficulty in the evangelical Church is that we have been trying to *think* our way into God. Nothing could be more futile and frustrating.

It is only through grace that you can have the fullness of the knowledge of God, but of God Himself can no man think. You cannot think around Him, equal to Him or up to Him. But that hunger for Him in your heart will reach out and search until it finds the object of His love, which is God Himself.

How then can we know God? How can we pierce the cloud of darkness and be smote with a sharp dart of longing love? It is the longing for God without any other motive than reaching God Himself. Many have come up short and are satisfied with the works of God and even theology. Certainly, thought is necessary and right, but it ultimately is powerless because the seeking goes beyond the realm of the intellect. You cannot get through to God with your head. William Cowper's hymn "The Light and Glory of the Word" reflects this:

> The Spirit breathes upon the Word,
> And brings the truth to sight;
> Precepts and promises afford
> A sanctifying light.
>
> A glory gilds the sacred page,
> Majestic like the sun:
> It gives a light to every age;
> It gives, but borrows none.
>
> The hand that gave it still supplies
> The gracious light and heat:
> His truths upon the nations rise;
> They rise, but never set.
>
> Let everlasting thanks be Thine
> For such a bright display
> As makes a world of darkness shine
> With beams of heavenly day.
>
> My soul rejoices to pursue
> The steps of Him I love,
> Till glory break upon my view
> In brighter worlds above.

A Mighty Infilling

Although it happened unintentionally, the Scriptures have become for some a substitute for God. The Bible has become a barrier between them and God. "We have our Bible," they say with a certain amount of pride, "and we need nothing more." Examine their lives and you may discover that the Bible has not really made an impact on their lifestyles. Remember, it is one thing to believe the Bible but something else altogether to allow the Bible, through the ministry of the Holy Spirit, to impact and change your life.

One problem some have is to believe that if they read it in the Bible, they have already experienced it. It is one thing to read about the new birth in the Bible and quite another thing to be born from above by the Spirit of the living God. It is one thing to read about being filled with the Holy Spirit and quite another thing to experience the mighty infilling of the Holy Spirit that radically changes our life to a life of adoring wonder and amazement at the things of God. Reading and experiencing are two quite different things.

Apart from the Holy Spirit breathing upon it, the Bible can be a useless thing, just another book of literature. It may be fine literature, but there is something infinitely more valuable than the Bible.

Appropriate the Promises

We might remember singing a little Sunday School chorus that says, "Every promise in the Book is mine." But we neglect to realize that it is one thing to believe a promise and quite another thing to appropriate it into our lives. It is like a man stumbling in the darkness of the night, not able to see his hand in front of his face. His companion asks, "How can you see in this darkness?"

"It's all right," the man might say, "I have a flashlight in my pocket." Simply having a flashlight in your pocket does not light your way until you pull it out and turn it on. Simply believing the Bible does no good until we pull those promises of God out of the Bible and by faith appropriate them into our lives.

One little saying that goes around in evangelical circles is "God said it, I believe it, and that settles it." The problem with that is that if you do not believe something to the extent that you appropriate it in your life, do you really believe it? The Bible exhorts us to "walk in the light." But the light has no value whatsoever unless we are walking in it.

Separate Yourself

Some Christians have come to the point where they have talked their way about as far as they can get. They will never get any further with their head, so they might as well put it to rest. It is the hungry heart that will finally penetrate the veil and encounter God, but this will be in the lonely recesses of the heart, far from things in the natural world. This is where God will meet us—far from the maddening crowd.

Study the Old Testament Tabernacle and you will get an idea of what I mean. The high priest had to go through various stages until he finally separated himself from the natural light and entered into the presence of Jehovah. In that presence was the supernatural illumination of God's presence.

With nothing to protect him but the blood offering and the assurance of God's promise, the priest stood there in the presence of that supernatural shining. He stood there alone. Nobody could accompany him into that shining place.

This is very hard for modern-day Christians to grasp. We live in an era of helps. At no other time in history have there been more helps with the Christian life than today. It is a strange oxymoron that the more Bible helps we have, the less spiritual power we exhibit. That's because these helps can only go so far.

The teacher can teach a student to read, but that is really as far as she can go. What that student reads is really up to him. The teacher can help him so far; then he is on his own. This is true throughout life. There are some things in life that must be done by ourselves. Nobody can help us. Nobody can assist us along the way. That is why there is a breakdown in evangelical circles today. We want to rely on each other. We want to exercise the "ministry of helps." We are nothing unless we have a crowd around us, not realizing that to penetrate into the very presence of God is a very lonely journey.

Although there may be many companions along the way as we live the crucified life, nobody can experience our experiences for us. Moreover, we cannot experience anybody else's experiences. It boils down to simply this: God and us. And when we come into His presence, we come by ourselves. Christian fellowship is wonderful, but there comes a time when even that becomes a hindrance. You will be alone even when a crowd surrounds you. Although there were 3,000 converted through Peter's preaching on the day of Pentecost, each was converted alone. When the Holy Ghost came at Pentecost, it did not set upon them en masse. It set upon them individually, and each went through the experience as if he were the only one present.

You probably want to help others, so do it as far as you can, but God wants you to press through to where there is no natural light to help you. You cannot lean on anything natural when you're in God's presence.

Make Up Your Own Mind

A man once wrote in an evangelical magazine, "I have accepted the doctrines of such and such a denomination." He had allowed somebody else to make up his mind for him. That is why millions of people are contented Catholics (or Methodists or Presbyterians), because somebody does their thinking for them. Somebody assures them, says a word of love and consolation, and has done all the thinking for them. Someone higher up has taken up all the responsibility. All they have to do is obey without question.

I do not mean to be unkind. I only say this is why certain religious denominations can hold their people and never say, "It is you and God." You have to find God "as the hart panteth after the water brooks" (Ps. 42:1). You have to seek God alone. I will help you with Scripture and do my best to help you, but when He meets you, it will be by yourself. You cannot take the authority of somebody else. Nobody can come and say, "All right, it's done. I hereby now as of today, at this hour, declare you are all right."

A young Christian earnestly seeking God once said to me, "I think you've got it." Thank God, I knew better, because that could have been the end of me. Our desire is for everyone to cry out to God and look in His direction with nothing but the naked intent of seeking God Himself. I want God and I want nothing more.

Some believe that "justified through His redemption" is simply a figure of speech. I believe that when Jesus Christ said, "He that receiveth me, receiveth him that sent me" (Matt. 10:40), He meant that *He* had received me. And I am not going to be shown up by some bright scholar who tells me that Jesus' words were some illustration drawn from a foreign court of law. Maybe the illustration or figure was drawn from there, but in back of that figure of speech, bolstering it, is the hard-core reality in my life and future and hope for that to be more than an illustration.

It is a glorious solid hard-core fact, hard on the rock of ages. For Jesus Christ removed all legal hindrances of why I should not to go to heaven. But I believe a holy God must run His universe according to His holy law. If He runs His kingdom according to His holy law, I don't care, because I have broken every one of His laws either in intent or on purpose. So justification must be somewhere. Redemption must be somewhere. Something has to be done legally to permit me to have God and for God to have me. And it *has* been done. Thank God, it has been done!

Believe God

There are times when all we can do is believe God and what He says. Believe Him in love. The author of *The Cloud of Unknowing* says, "God Himself can no man think. . . . He may well be loved, but not thought." Almighty God created the universe, and His presence overflows into immense degrees and can never be surrounded by that little thing we call our head, our intellect. He knows that all we can do is seek but never arrive at God.

Empty Yourself

One phenomenon of nature is that there is no such thing as a vacuum. It does not exist in nature, and neither does one exist in the spiritual world. As long as a vessel is filled with something, nothing else can come in. And here is where a spiritual law comes into play. As long as there is something in my life, God cannot fill it.

If I empty out half of my life, God can only fill half. And my spiritual life would be diluted with the things of the natural man. This seems to be the condition of many Christians today. They are willing to get rid of some things in their lives, and God comes and fills them as far as He can. But until they are willing to give up everything and put everything on the altar, as it were, God cannot fill their entire lives.

One of the strange things about God is that He will come in as far as we allow Him. I have often said that a Christian is as full of the Holy Spirit as he wants to be. We can beg to be filled with the Holy Spirit. We can talk about it, but until we are willing to empty ourselves, we will never have the fullness of the Holy Spirit in our lives. God will fill as much of us as we allow Him to fill.

As we create a sort of vacuum in our lives, we are in fact inviting the Holy Spirit to come rushing in. On the day of Pentecost, there was the sound "of a rushing mighty wind" (Acts 2:2). The reason for that was that those disciples stood before God, emptied of everything. They had room for nothing but God. And when they presented themselves as empty vessels before the Lord, He rushed mightily to fill them.

No matter what generation you look at or what century you study, you will discover a consistency in what the Holy Spirit is saying and doing. From the day of Pentecost on down to this present hour, there is only one thing on the Holy Spirit's mind: to fill the Church with His glorious presence. His message is simply, "Empty yourself, and I, the Holy Spirit, will come fill you to overflowing."

A Self-Deliverance

Some people might say, "Pastor, I would be a better Christian if I had a better pastor." I wish it could be so. But you know that would not be the case, because the better pastor you had, the more you would become a spiritual parasite and lean on him. Often the most spiritual people attend churches where the pastor cannot preach his way out of a wet paper bag. The reason is because they have no help from the pulpit, so they have to learn to lean on God. If you get too much help from the pulpit, you tend to become a parasite and lean on your pastor. I believe in the priesthood of believers.

Get delivered from yourself. When you are stuck so far down in the mud that only God can pull you out, it will be a sound that can be heard a block away. Stop thinking that you are somebody. Stop thinking that you can make it as a blessed theologian. You know just so much. As someone once said, "God by love may be known and we may be holy, but taught, never." Be careful not to try to enter into the deeper life by your wits or your imagination. Do not try to look to God by yourself and keep God in your own heart. I do not mean it is not all right to go to an altar to pray. That is another matter. I am talking about the loneliness of the soul that is cut out of the crowd.

Even as the woman pushed herself toward Jesus and was crushed in the crowds that were touching Him on every side, she continued to push forward and finally touched the hem of His clothes. He said, "Who touched me?" (Mark 5:31; Luke 8:45).

Jesus' disciples pointed out that He was crowded on every side, but Jesus said, "I didn't mean that. I meant who touched me in faith" (see Luke 8:46). The disciples were merely jostled. They were with Jesus, but they just got jostled. But the woman who was by herself, separate, pushed toward Him and was touched by Him in faith and love.

We need to have our hearts healed. We need to have God's anointing on our hearts. There is an old hymn by A. B. Simpson that attests to this fact:

Yes, there's balm, there is balm in Gilead;
There's a great Physician there!
Let us bring Him all our sickness,
Cast upon Him all our care.

The crucified life is a blessed but lonely life that no man can walk for someone else.

The Light and Glory of the Word
William Cowper (1731–1800)

The Spirit breathes upon the word,
And brings the truth to sight;
Precepts and promises afford
A sanctifying light.

A glory gilds the sacred page,
Majestic like the sun;
It gives a light to every age,
It gives, but borrows none.

The hand that gave it still supplies
The gracious light and heat;
His truths upon the nations rise,
They rise, but never set.

Let everlasting thanks be thine,
For such a bright display,
As makes a world of darkness shine
With beams of heavenly day.

My soul rejoices to pursue
The steps of Him I love,
Till glory break upon my view
In brighter worlds above.

PART II

· · · · · · · · · · · · ·

THE DYNAMICS OF THE CRUCIFIED LIFE

5

THE CASE FOR GOING ON INTO THE PROMISED LAND

Moses my servant is dead; now therefore arise,
go over this Jordan, thou, and all this people, unto the land
which I do give to them, even to the children of Israel.
Every place that the sole of your foot shall tread upon,
that have I given unto you, as I said unto Moses.

JOSHUA 1:2-3

You can always test the quality of religious teaching by the enthusiastic reception it receives from unsaved men. If the natural man receives it enthusiastically, it is not of the Spirit of God. Paul says plainly that the natural man cannot know spiritual things. To him, spiritual things are plain foolishness (see 1 Cor. 2:14).

There is a type of religious teaching understood, received by and perfectly logical to the natural man. But the natural man does not know that which is of the Spirit of God. He does not have the faculty to receive it.

The natural man is of this world. He may be in perfect health and have an IQ of 180. He may be as handsome as a Greek statue or, if a woman, a perfect example of fine womanhood. Or he might be a perfect example of the young American. The natural man, though he is in this state, is unblessed and out of grace.

Contrary to the natural man is the spiritual man. This is the Christian who is mature in his faith, who is led, taught and controlled by the Holy Spirit, and to whom the Spirit of God can speak.

Then there is the carnal man. The carnal man is the immature Christian. He is no longer a natural man, for he has been renewed by the grace of God and is in a state of grace, but he is not spiritual. He is halfway in between the two. He has been regenerated but is not advancing in his spiritual life. He is not influenced or led by the Holy Spirit but rather is controlled by his lower nature.

Of the three types, it is the spiritual man who is living the crucified life. He is indwelt, led, taught, influenced and controlled by the Holy Spirit.

Old Testament Prototypes

The Old Testament prototype of the natural man—those who are not in a state of grace—was Israel in Egypt. Four hundred years the Israelites had been in Egypt, and a major part of that time they had been in bondage to Pharaoh. Then came Moses who, through blood and atonement and power, led the children of Israel out of Egypt with the Red Sea closing between Israel and Egypt. That corresponded to the new birth.

Regeneration, or rebirth, makes the natural man a Christian, which takes him out of nature and puts him in a state of grace. Israel came out of Egypt and went across the sea, and the sea closed behind them and the enemy died. Israel for the first time in 400 years was a free nation, redeemed by blood and by power.

This is like the Christian who for all of his lifetime has been subject to bondages of various kinds—chains and shackles and manacles have been upon his spirit. Now, through the blood of the Lamb, the power of the Spirit, he is brought out of Egypt, and the Red Sea closes after him. We used to sing the hymn "I've Turned My Back upon the World" by Elisha A Hoffman:

I've turned my back upon the world
With all its idle pleasures,
And set my heart on better things,
On higher, holier treasures;
No more its glitter and its glare,
And vanity shall blind me;
I've crossed the separating line,
And left the world behind me.

These words describe exactly what happened to Israel in the land of Canaan. It was God's benevolent intention that the natural man in bondage in Egypt should come out of Egypt and make an 11-day journey to the holy land offered to Abraham by God in covenant. The holy land—variously called the Promised Land, the land of promise, and Canaan—was to be the homeland of Israel.

Israel was not only to be out of Egypt but also to be in the holy land, their spiritual homeland. God brought them out so that He might bring them in. This point has been lost in our teaching today. God brings us out, not that we may be out, but that we may be brought in.

God saves a criminal not so that he might tell about it once a year for the next 40 years but so that he might become a saint. God takes him out of his bondage that He might lead that person into the Promised Land. And the farther in the man goes, the less he will have to say about where he used to be. It is not the mark of spirituality when I talk at length about what I used to be. Israel wanted to forget what she used to be and remembered only occasionally to thank God for her deliverance.

Today, we magnify what we used to be and write books to tell the world about it. Paul said, "Those things ought not even to be mentioned among the people of God" (see Eph. 5:12). They are not even to be mentioned in conversation. God brought you out, but He does not leave you in limbo. He brought you out so that He might bring you in, and that was the will of God.

After God brought Israel out of Egypt, He showed them, after an 11-day march, the Promised Land. The enemy could have been driven out, and they could have had the holy land of promise God had given to them centuries before. They would not be stealing it. They would be occupying it as their proper possession. God, who owned it, had given it to Abraham and his seed after him. Abraham's seed had been driven out and into Egypt. God was now bringing Israel back to put them in the land. They were not to be usurpers—not to take the land— but to occupy the land, which was properly theirs by a gift of the One who owned it: God.

Metaphorically, God brought the Israelites out of sin so that He might bring them into the spiritual life. The Israelites' march was a God-blessed, God-hovered-over and Shekinah-enlightened journey straight through to the Holy Land. When they arrived in the land of promise from which Abraham had come centuries before, they were to be spiritual men. They represent an Old Testament prototype of the spiritual man.

The Natural Man

If you are a natural man, no matter how learned, how talented, how handsome or how desirable you are, you do not know a thing about God and you do not know a thing about the spiritual life. You do not have the faculties to know it.

If a man who is stone deaf sits reading while a Mozart Symphony is playing, you would not blame him because he would rather read than listen to the music. He does not have the ability to enjoy the music. The ability you have in you to listen to the symphony is dead in him.

Or if you were in an art gallery looking at paintings and there was a man completely blind sitting on the bench, you would not say, "Why is that Philistine just sitting there? Why doesn't he get up and look at the paintings?" He does not have the ability to look at paintings. The ability you have to look at paintings is dead in him.

No matter who you are or how learned or religious you are, if you have not been regenerated, renewed, made over, brought to the light by the quickening of the Holy Spirit, you cannot know God. You cannot know spiritual things at all; you can only know the history of spiritual things. Any enthusiasm you have for religion is but an illusion.

The Spiritual Man

Paul says that we Christians who are quickened to life—who are God's children, who are not in the state of nature anymore but in a state of grace—but who continue without progress year after year, wander spiritually instead of moving straight ahead. Sometimes we may get a little closer to Egypt than to the Holy Land; then we again get a little closer to the Holy Land; then back to Egypt. So we swing on our pendulum, back and forth, occasionally looking over the sea and remembering that we used to be slaves.

Then we go to a prayer meeting or some revival, put out our arms, and we move so close to the Holy Land that we can almost touch it. But we are not going to either place. We are not going back into the world, and we are not going to push on into the spiritual life. So back and forth we go, swinging between the old world we came from and the new world where we ought to be.

To continue without progress year after year is to develop a sort of chronic heart disease. Your heart becomes harder and harder as time passes. The best time to plunge into the deeper spiritual life is when you are a young Christian and have enthusiasm and can form deep-seated habits.

If I were to try to learn Japanese at my age, it would almost be hopeless. I could learn to read and write it. But I could never speak it well enough to be understood, because I have been around too long and my tongue and lips and palate have been too used to only having to form English words. All the little twists, turns and slurs of the English tongue fit my mouth. The older I get, the harder it is for me to learn a new language. However, a young person can pick it up and rattle it off in no time flat. The younger you are, the easier it is to learn and speak a new language because over time, habits have a tendency to harden you.

The Carnal Man

Now, what about the carnal man? The carnal man is the immature Christian who does not go on or advance. He is slowed in His spiritual development and is not influenced or controlled by the Holy Spirit but rather by his lower nature.

When Israel came to Kadesh-Barnea after marching a little while in the direction of the Promised Land, they stopped (see Num. 13–14). Moses said to them, in effect, "We're about to enter into the land that has been the object of your hope since God brought you out of Egypt."

Israel responded, "We're a little afraid. So send up 12 men to spy on the land." So Moses sent 12 men to examine the land and report back to determine whether they could take it or not. When the spies came back, all of them reported that it was an exceedingly good land. There was water there. To people in that country, water amounted to riches untold. It was more valuable than silver and gold and diamonds. So to report that this was an exceedingly good land in which there was much water was equivalent to saying that it was a sort of paradise.

They found grapes so large that it took two men to carry one branch between them. They found dates, which would have been our equivalent of sugar, candy, preserves, marmalade jelly and sodas. Everybody has his sweet tooth, and they had their dates. Figs and dates were probably the sweetest part of their diet. And there were pomegranates. Pomegranates are berries but are near enough to citrus fruit to have been classified as it. They are literally packed with vitamins. They would be well worth having.

Then there was milk and honey. When the Bible says "a land flowing with milk and honey," this is not careless language (Exod. 3:8). There were a great many bees in the land. There was so much honey that the trees could not hold it all, so it literally dripped down on great rocks. And there was abundant milk from sheep and goats. This land was so different from Egypt, the land they had come from only a little while before.

Now, after 10 of these 12 men came back and reported what the country was like, they nevertheless said, "We advise you not to go up into the land because although it is an exceedingly good land with lots of water, grapes, figs, pomegranates, milk and honey, the people are large and strong. There are giants there and their cities are great and walled up to heaven."

A land with brooks of water, grapes, figs, pomegranates, milk and honey does not sound to me as if it were being eaten up by its giant inhabitants. Besides that, the spies had not stayed long enough to watch the inhabitants eat up anything. The 10 men were simply frightened and filled with unbelief and advised against going on.

"Let's stay here in the wilderness," was their advice. "We're free of Egypt, thank God, and are not slaves anymore. We are in the wilderness, and while it isn't the best, we will settle for it rather than go up against those giants in that wonderful promised homeland."

Then Caleb and Joshua stepped to the head of the line and said to Moses, "We are ready to go in. Pay no attention to these pessimists. We can easily take the land, and there will be bread for us. The land belongs to us, our father's God gave it to us— gave it to Abraham, our father—and it's ours. Let's go take it."

Caleb and Joshua told of the rich advantages in the land and were unwilling to allow the large strong giants in the walled cities to keep them out.

All the teaching today about the Church being the perfect democracy and about how there should be no leaders is just plain poppycock with nothing in the Old or New Testaments to support it. Twelve leaders were sent to spy out the land, and the people were more or less dependent on what those leaders said. Just as you and I are similarly dependent in this democracy upon our leaders in Washington to a large extent. And in the Church of Christ, it is the same.

The people heard the unfavorable report of the 10 men; that is, the majority report. Caleb and Joshua gave the minority report, but they were only two. The people wept and fell down in front of their tent doors, wishing they had not come out of Egypt. They complained to Moses and said, "Would to God we were back in Egypt."

All the Israelites could see was walled cities and giants. They could not see grapes or goats with their great utters dripping with milk or trees drooling sweet honey down onto the grass. They could not see the rolling grasslands and the brooks and rivers. All they could see were the giants in the land. They forgot that God said, "Go up and I'll give it to you." So they said, "You'll kill our poor women. You'll kill our children."

This is always the unspiritual man's argument: "I've got to think about my family. I've got a family after all, brother, and God wants us to be wise, and I can't push this too far. I can't become too spiritual because I've got to think about my family. I can't subject my wife and children to difficulties. I can't lay burdens on them." Always pleasing their wives and family, such a man forgets that the best heritage a husband can leave his family is the memory that he was a good man. A spiritual woman also faces stumbling blocks. Her family may fight her with hot language, scold her with sarcastic speech, oppose her and make her feel like an idiot. However, a spiritual woman will walk quietly away, sadder but wiser, and will admit that the best heritage she can leave her family is that she was a good woman.

Had these Israelites only believed, they could have taken all their wives and families into the Holy Land within a few hours. They would have had all that land. Instead, for 40 years, they wandered in the desert. They had been so afraid that those wives and children were going to be killed if they went into that land that they ended up walking for 40 years, wandering round and round and round in the desert. Now swinging back near to Egypt where they had been, now a wide swing close to the Promised Land where they should be. Back again to Egypt where they were not, then around again, then by the loop again near to where they ought to be.

They wandered for 40 years until those children were grown to middle age and those women were dead. Forty years of it because the men had whimpered and said, "We can't go. It would cost us too much. We can't mistreat our families. We have to be with our families on Sunday nights and Wednesday nights and all during the missionary convention. We have to be with our families. We can't take a chance of our children becoming juvenile delinquents."

The best way for a husband to save his family from delinquency is to show them an example of a man who loves God uncompromisingly. A man who seeks to be spiritual, even though it costs him his blood. A man who doesn't listen to the devil's ruse: "You give more than you should to the Lord's work already, and if you seek to become a spiritual man, you will harm your family."

Israel wandered in the desert for 40 years by God's judgment. God said, "Doubtless ye shall not come into the land" (Num. 14:30). Their fear of death and their doubts and complaining displeased God because the people brought "a slander to the land" (Num. 14:36).

Every man who stands in the shadows and slanders the deeper spiritual life is slandering the sunshine. Every man who refuses to enter into the holy life is in the wilderness, slandering the homeland of the soul. For 40 years, Israel wandered aimlessly about. God was with them. He did not destroy them; rather, He let them die one at a time. Occasionally, He would punish them, but He did not destroy them as a nation.

Spiritual Failures

I refuse to be discouraged about anything, but it gives me a heavy heart to walk among Christians who have wandered for 40 long years in the wilderness, not going back to sin but not going on into the holy life. Wandering in an aimless circle, sometimes a little warmer, sometimes a little colder, sometimes a little holier and sometimes very unholy, but never going on. Habits have been acquired and are hard to break, and it makes it almost certain that they will live and die spiritual failures. To me this is a terrible thing.

A man decides to be a lawyer and spends years studying law and finally puts out his shingle. He soon finds something in his temperament that makes it impossible for him to make good as a lawyer. He is a complete failure. He is 50 years old, was admitted to the bar when he was 30, and 20 years later, he has not been able to make a living as a lawyer. As a lawyer, he is a failure.

A businessman buys a business and tries to operate it. He does everything that he knows how to do but just cannot make it go. Year after year the ledger shows red, and he is not making a profit. He borrows what he can, has a little spirit and a little hope, but that spirit and hope die and he goes broke. Finally, he sells out, hopelessly in debt, and is left a failure in the business world.

A woman is educated to be a teacher but just cannot get along with the other teachers. Something in her constitution or temperament will not allow her to get along with children or young people. So after being shuttled from one school to another, she finally gives up, goes somewhere and takes a job running a stapling machine. She just cannot teach and is a failure in the education world.

I have known ministers who thought they were called to preach. They prayed and studied and learned Greek and Hebrew, but somehow they just could not make the public want to listen to them. They just couldn't do it. They were failures in the congregational world.

It is possible to be a Christian and yet be a failure. This is the same as Israel in the desert, wandering around. The Israelites were God's people, protected and fed, but they were failures. They were not where God meant them to be. They compromised. They were halfway between where they used to be and where they ought to be. And that describes many of the Lord's people. They live and die spiritual failures.

I am glad God is good and kind. Failures can crawl into God's arms, relax and say, "Father, I made a mess of it. I'm a spiritual failure. I haven't been out doing evil things exactly, but here I am, Father, and I'm old and ready to go and I'm a failure."

Our kind and gracious heavenly Father will not say to that person, "Depart from me—I never knew you," because that person has believed and does believe in Jesus Christ. The individual has simply been a failure all of his life. He is ready for death and ready for heaven. I wonder if that is what Paul, the man of God, meant when he said:

[No] other foundation can [any] man lay than that is laid, which is Jesus Christ. Now if any man build upon this foundation gold, silver, precious stones, wood, hay, stubble; every man's work shall be made manifest: for the day shall declare it, because it shall be revealed by fire; and the fire shall try every man's work of what sort it is. If any man's work abide which he hath built thereupon, he should receive a reward. If any man's work shall be burned, he shall suffer loss: but he himself shall be saved; yet so as by fire (1 Cor. 3:11-15).

I think that's what it means, all right. We ought to be the kind of Christian that cannot only save our souls but also save our lives. When Lot left Sodom, he had nothing but the garments on his back. Thank God, he got out. But how much better it would have been if he had said farewell at the gate and had camels loaded with his goods. He could have gone out with his head up, chin out, saying good riddance to old Sodom. How much better he could have marched away from there with his family. And when he settled in a new place, he could have had "an abundant entrance" (see 2 Pet. 1:11).

Thank God, *you* are going to make it. But do you want to make it in the way you have been acting lately? Wandering, roaming aimlessly? When there is a place where Jesus will pour "the oil of gladness" on our heads, a place sweeter than any other in the entire world, the blood-bought mercy seat (Ps. 45:7; Heb. 1:9)? It is the will of God that you should enter the holy of holies, live under the shadow of the mercy seat, and go out from there and always come back to be renewed and recharged and re-fed. It is the will of God that you live by the mercy seat, living a separated, clean, holy, sacrificial life—a life of continual spiritual difference. Wouldn't that be better than the way you are doing it now?

We're Marching to Zion
Isaac Watts (1674–1748)

Come, we that love the Lord,
And let our joys be known;
Join in a song with sweet accord,
Join in a song with sweet accord
And thus surround the throne,
And thus surround the throne.

We're marching to Zion,
Beautiful, beautiful Zion;
We're marching upward to Zion,
The beautiful city of God.

Let those refuse to sing
Who never knew our God;
But children of the heavenly King,
But children of the heavenly King
May speak their joys abroad,
May speak their joys abroad.

The hill of Zion yields
A thousand sacred sweets
Before we reach the heavenly fields,
Before we reach the heavenly fields,
Or walk the golden streets,
Or walk the golden streets.

Then let our songs abound,
And every tear be dry;
We're marching through Emmanuel's ground,
We're marching through Emmanuel's ground,
To fairer worlds on high,
To fairer worlds on high.

6

A Discontent with the Status Quo

For whosoever will save his life shall lose it; but whosoever shall lose his life for my sake and the gospel's, the same shall save it. For what shall it profit a man, if he shall gain the whole world, and lose his own soul? Or what shall a man give in exchange for his soul? Whosoever therefore shall be ashamed of me and of my words in this adulterous and sinful generation; of him also shall the Son of man be ashamed, when he cometh in the glory of his Father with the holy angels.

MARK 8:35-38

Following salvation, the Holy Spirit rises up early, encourages the new Christian forward and urges him to urge others to go forward. The idea of there being a better Christian life than most people know is neither a modern development nor a modern idea. It can be traced all the way back to the Old Testament and the experience of Israel.

The history of Israel is indeed an illustration of this truth. God led the Israelites out of Egypt miraculously, through the Red Sea, into the wilderness and on through and across the River Jordan into the Holy Land. All the way, Israel was led by a cloud during the day and a fiery pillar by night. The people drank water from a rock and their food was angels' food, which came down from above. The whole history of Israel is filled with one miracle right after another.

But it was not long before changes took place. These changes did not happen overnight but occurred gradually, over many years. Slowly but surely the Israelites moved from the center to the perimeter. They soon fell prey to externalism. Instead of being led by God day by day, they became content to live by rote. They did today what they had done yesterday because they did it the day before.

The Fire of Internalism

This is where the prophets of the Old Testament stepped in and called Israel back to the center, to following Jehovah.

It is the same with the Church today. God wants us to have content, but we are satisfied with mere words. When we can simply say words, we in a measure satisfy our consciences. We love form without worship, but God wants worship whether or not it has form.

Like Israel of old, the Church today is satisfied with words, ceremonies and forms. The words the prophets spoke to the Israelites are as true for us today: God wants us to have content, love and worship—internal spiritual reality of that inner fire of God.

Once this fire of internalism dies down, externalism begins developing. It is at this time that God sends prophets and holy seers to rebuke the hollow form of worship that is merely ritual and to plead for what we call the deeper life, or the crucified life. This Christian life is something deeper than the average life among Christians and is nearer to ideal New Testament Christianity, which should be the norm.

It is not difficult to see in the history of the Church a gradual shift toward externalism. Occasionally God bolsters His people with a mighty revival. He begins to pour out His power, and people are stirred and break away from externalism and the empty hollow rituals that are a big part of their worship. They break through to an experience with God that is above the norm and what they had known up to that point. Many of the great hymns of the Church have come out of these great moves of God.

The Mechanics of Institutionalism

As great and wonderful as these moves of God are, however, it does not take long to drift slowly back into externalism. Once externalism gets a good hold, institutionalism begins to take over. Then follows form, ceremony and tradition, and the church begins to celebrate what once was and those who once were. An external ceremony replaces the inner fire of the Holy Spirit.

The prophets of God objected to this. In the book of Malachi, there is one of the loveliest, tenderest little passages imaginable. It is the testimony of the prophet Malachi 400 years before the Maccabees and before Christ came. Malachi was the last prophet to appear to Israel to bring them the sacred word of God. Malachi rebuked and warned in every way he knew. He exhorted and urged the people who had drifted into externalism and were satisfied with the whirling machinery and the motion of the pieces and parts, but cared nothing about the beating heart of worship and the life within it. Here is Malachi's tender little testimony about a few of those whom we would say saw the deeper Christian life:

> Then they that feared the LORD spake often one to another: and the LORD hearkened, and heard it, and a book of remembrance was written before him for them that feared the LORD, and that thought upon his name. And they shall be mine, saith the LORD of hosts,

in that day when I make up my jewels; and I will spare them, as a man spareth his own son that serveth him. Then shall ye return, and discern between the righteous and the wicked, between him that serveth God and him that serveth him not (Mal. 3:16-18).

This company of people was not many, but they were the called. They feared the Lord and spoke often to each other, and the Lord was pleased, so Malachi wrote about them in the book. That was worship according to the Old Testament.

The Faltering of the New Testament Church

We then come over into the New Testament with all the wonders of the incarnation, the crucifixion, the resurrection of Christ and the pouring out of the Holy Spirit at Pentecost. The Church began as Israel before her had begun, in a blaze of life and power. The Church was known for its simplicity, along with faith, love, purity and worship.

But again, the inner fire was eventually reduced to the ashes of externalism. So, again, God sent His prophets. Saint Augustine met God in a marvelous and wonderful way. While living in the framework of the organized Church, Augustine knew God with trembling rapture and worship, and he wrote about it in his magnificent and justly famous books.

Then came Bernard of Cluny in the twelfth century. He dreamed that someday he might visit Rome, and after much effort and preparation, he succeeded in realizing his dream. He went to Rome and visited the very headquarters of the Church. There he saw what was going on. He saw the pomp and circumstance of the priests. He saw that form and ceremony, with very little true spirituality anywhere, even among those in high positions, had taken over. This so broke his heart that he went back to his little valley and hid himself away and wrote his famous "The Celestial Country," one of the most rapturous pieces of literature ever penned by any human being on this earth. It was a mighty cry of a man hungry after God, protesting against all the formality—and particularly against the corruption—he saw in the Church.

Saint Francis of Assisi came along also protesting this formality in the Church. I think most invariably his order grew out of a great revival in the heart of this man. He formed his order that he might give spiritual religion a chance to live again. He had no more than died and gone to sleep with his fathers when formality and externalism took over again. This has been the history of the Church down the years.

These men I have named rebuked and pleaded for a life that was real. God has always had His men to plead and earnestly long that they might be holy and might have within themselves what they knew the Bible taught.

The Appearance of the Protestant Church

So far, I have been giving examples from the Roman Church, but now let me come to the Protestant Church. I point out to you quite sadly, as I must, that this shift toward externalism is just as strong within the Protestant Church as it ever was in Israel or in the Church before Luther's time. The temptation to go outward toward words, traditions, forms, customs and habits is too much to resist. We carry on our backs whole loads of traditions that have no place in the work of God. Jesus taught, "In vain they do worship me, teaching for doctrines the commandments of men" (Matt. 15:9). If we can allow a word to stand for the deed, we will do the word and not do the deed.

Tarnished Stained-Glass Windows

Whenever I am in a city, I make time to visit some of the cathedrals and great religious centers, whether Catholic or Protestant. In one city, a man took me around and told me, "These windows that you see are exact replicas of a famous cathedral in Europe. The artist went to Europe, copied with exquisite precision the stained-glass windows of that famous cathedral and brought them back to this country. This is a perfect replica of such and such cathedral, all of these beautiful stained-glass windows."

Then he said something rather shocking. "I want to point out something to you. You notice here and there are what appear to be spots and splotches? Notice how down along the edge, close to the frame, there's a bit of discoloration?"

I noticed this and told him so. "These windows are hundreds of years old and have stood for centuries, as nations and kingdoms rose and fell, and they naturally got washed only by the rains. Now they've collected on themselves a certain tarnish and discoloration and the dust of the centuries. There were those who believed that the dust and discoloration actually improved and mellowed the windows and made them look better than they were before. So when the artist went over to copy them, they did not wash the windows nor did they try to copy the windows without the dirt. But they copied dirt and windows so that what we have here is not only the artistry and the stained-glass windows of the cathedral, but we have in addition, perfectly reproduced, the centuries-old dust that gathered on the windows."

Those windows are a perfect illustration of what happened with Israel, what happened with the Early Church of Christ, and what happened with every order that has ever been established and every new denomination that has ever been born out of an earnest desire to bring men to God. They become like those tarnished stained-glass windows. The dust of the centuries gets on them and becomes a part of their beliefs and part of their practices, so they are hardly able to tell which is of God and which is simply the accumulation of tarnish from the centuries.

That is exactly what we have done in our time. Do not imagine for a minute that we have been without our prophets and seers who have stood and warned us and tried to bring us back to God. God still has those who are not content with superficial worship. They are not all of one denomination, but they are discontent with surface religion. They long to recapture the true inwardness of the faith, and they insist upon reality. They do not want anything artificial; they want to know that whatever they have is real. They would rather it be small and real than large and unreal. "A living dog is better than a dead lion," as it is said in the Old Testament (Eccles. 9:4).

And so it is better to have a little church that is real than a big church that is artificial. It is better to have a simple religion that is real than to have a great ornate ceremony that is only hollow and empty.

New Testament Exclusivity

Unfortunately, there are those who want nothing apart from the New Testament. They live among God's people everywhere. I find them here and there in my travels and I believe there are some in almost every religious group. Remember this: You and I are brought to the Bible, which is our rock from which we drink our water. This is our manna. This is our blueprint upon which we build our cathedral. This is our guide through the desert in the wilderness. This is our all in all, and we want nothing else. The people that I'm talking about want nothing except what is in the New Testament.

The difficulty down the years, as a rule, was not that men taught wrong doctrine, but that they did not live up to the doctrine they taught. This did not become apparent until a reformer or a prophet came along to rebuke the Church for holding the doctrine without having the inward reality of it. When such men like John Wesley came along, they did not try to straighten out the Church or correct its doctrines. They insisted on a witness in the heart that the things being taught are real in us. We follow these reformers and prophets because they found reality in the Word of God for their own hearts and they wanted nothing outside of the Bible. They simply wanted what the Bible had for them.

These of which I speak had only one source of riches, and all those riches are in Christ. For them, Jesus Christ was enough. It was not Christ plus something else. Jesus Christ was their all in all, fully sufficient. Those who seek the deeper Christian life and those who want the riches that are in Christ Jesus the Lord seek no place, no wealth, no things, only Christ.

Coattail Riders

So many men these days are using religion as a source of wealth, fame, publicity or something else. They are using religion to get something for themselves. It is obvious that they are taking advantage of whatever happens to be current, riding the coattails of whatever new thing has come along. I have outlived innumerable sheaves of men who came along and tried to cash in on whatever was popular at the time.

While these men latched on to whatever was popular at the moment, I went right on preaching the gospel. I never preached to big crowds, at least not in my own church. But I preached a consistent Christ. This desire of wanting to get a following, to be well known, to get a reputation, is not for those who are living the crucified life. Those who walk and live the crucified life have no desire for these things and are willing to lose their reputations if they must in order to get on with God and go on to perfection. They seek no place, no wealth, no thing. Those who long after God will not turn their heads to be elected anywhere to anything. Only static Christians seek after high ecclesiastical positions. They want to be somebody before they die.

Occasionally I hear about some big shot in the eyes of the world who has died. Immediately I say to myself, *What now, brother? While you lived, you climbed the ladder of success, trampling other men down in the name of Christ and religion. Now you are dead. The worms will eat you; and your poor spotted, tarnished soul and you now face the Judge of all the earth. What now, man?*

The Crucified Life of God Seekers

Those living the crucified life do not seek place or wealth, fame or high positions. Rather, they want to know God and to be where Jesus is. Only to know Christ—that is all. Paul said, "Yea doubtless, and I count all things but loss for the excellency of the knowledge of Christ Jesus my Lord: for whom I have suffered the loss of all things, and do count them but dung, that I may win Christ" (Phil. 3:8).

The seekers after God are deeply dissatisfied with mere form. You cannot fool them with painted toys; they want content.

In *all* denominations everywhere, there are godly people seeking the face of Jesus. And kindness and charity lead me to say that I think some of them are over on the other side of the fence. For example, Thomas Merton was a seeker after God. I believe he was an example of those who have never left the ancient Roman Church and who know God and are seekers after God. I personally cannot see why they do not leave, but I believe there are a few other such people. So God has His people everywhere, known by the fact that they hate mere form. Even though they may go through with it, they have something within them that is bigger than all of that.

When Brother Lawrence (born Nicholas Herman), author of *The Practice of the Presence of God*, was in his monastery, he said:

> I learned to pray to God all by myself. I just talked to God all the time, everything I was doing—washing dishes, traveling, whatever I was doing—I was talking to my heavenly Father. I developed such a sense of God's presence around about me that I never lost it for 40 years. I did not need their forms. They told me set times to pray, and I did it. I was obedient. I prayed at set times, but it did not mean a thing anymore than it did at any other time. I had learned the inner secret of fellowship with God myself. I'd already found God and I was in communion with God all the time.

Brother Lawrence did what he was told and smiled, but he said it did not mean anything.

The Progress of the Average Christian Today

The average Christian's progress today is not sufficient to satisfy the longings of the seekers after God. They want something better than that. The average Christian today does not make much spiritual progress at all. He is converted, joins the Church, and five years later he is right back where he started. Ten years later, he is still where he was or he has even slipped back a little. That is not satisfactory to those who seek and thirst and hunger after God. "As the hart panteth after the water brooks, so panteth my soul after thee, O God. My soul thirsteth for God, for the living God" (Ps. 42:1-2). That is the testimony of a seeker after God. He is not going to let somebody's slow snail's progress keep him back.

Such seekers after God are impatient with the substitutes being offered today. When you do not have anything real inside of you, you try to get something on the outside that suggests something real. It is a well-known fact that when the fire goes out in the furnace, they paint the outside to make it look as if the fire was still there.

Unfortunately, the Church is the same. And this even includes evangelical and so-called full-gospel churches. Something from its heart has been lost, so bangles and dangles are used on the outside in order to pretend there is something real on the inside. But you cannot fool seekers after God with this kind of thing. They know better.

What have we come to, that the people of God are not shocked enough by Calvary, a man dying on a cross on a hill outside Jerusalem? And not just a man, but the Godman, dying for the sins of the world? Why does this leave them dull and unmoved? The recent outburst of modern theatrics has now taken over Protestantism. What started in the beginning as a small seed has grown; the dragon's seed has grown more dragons. The seekers of God do not like what's happening, and the hungry-hearted saints of God do not want it, so they read with great eagerness the lives of holy men in the devotional books from centuries past. But where is the *doing*?

The Fellowship of Prophets

I wonder if you have ever read *Sermons on the Song of Songs* or *On Loving God* by Bernard of Clairvaux. Have you ever read *Dark Night of the Soul* by Saint John of the Cross? Or *The Scale of Perfection* or *The Goad of Love* by Walter Hilton? Or *The Amending of Life* by Richard Rolle? Or *The Life of the Servant* or *A Little Book of Eternal*

Wisdom by Henry Suso? Or the great sermons by John Tauler and Meister Eckert? What about *The Imitation of Christ* by Thomas à Kempis? Or *Introduction to the Devout Life* by Francis de Sales? Or *The Cloud of Unknowing* or *The Letters of Samuel Rutherford* or the works of William Law or the letters of François Fénelon or the journal of John Fox? What about the writings of Nikolaus von Zinzendorf and Andrew Murray and John Wesley and A. B. Simpson? These men rose like the prophets of Israel and did not change their doctrine; they just professed it against the hollow externalisms of the world. They sought to recapture again the glory that was in Jesus Christ the Lord, of worship and prayer and the desire to be holy.

The men I have named formed a sacred fellowship through the years. But I do not find them, by any means, in the mainstream of evangelicalism today. There are men in evangelicalism today who are just ordinary men with no longing after God. They grind out their sermons week after week, take little trips here and there, fish and play golf and fool around and then come back and preach. They go on and spend their lives that way. But you cannot speak with them for long because there is nothing of substance to talk about after you have done a little chitchat business.

Not all preachers are that way. There are some whom you can speak with for hours on end and talk about God and Christ. These people are practical and clean and coolheaded and have no sympathy with false doctrines, and they keep away from extremes of excitement and fanaticism. They just want to know God and want to be holy. They want to seek the face of Jesus until they are aglow with His light.

I have described these men and women because what I really want to know is whether I described you. It is not a matter of how deep you have come, but do you have your diving suit on?

It is not how far the arrow has sped, but has the arrow left the bow? It is not that you are perfect but that you thirst after perfection. Or is your religion social? Are you satisfied with the once-on-Sunday sort of religion?

God has given you the wind, the rain, a body to contain your wonderful soul. He has given you an amazing mind and many fine abilities. He sustains you, holds you up, keeps your heart beating and waits to receive you yonder. But do you toss Him a crumb, so God gets what is left behind? Does God get only the tattered bits of your time, yet you say you are a follower of the Lamb? Do not fool yourself. You are not if you don't go deeper into the crucified life.

Are you weary of externalism, and do you long after God? I long after God. This is not old age talking, and this is not the result of anything I have been reading, except the Bible. This has been growing in me through the years. The only gratifying thing I have apart from my communion with God is the knowledge that I am not alone in my journey. God has His people everywhere who are in revolt against pretense, textualism, externalism and tradition. They want to seek God for Himself, as He is in the Scriptures, as revealed by the Holy Spirit.

God has His people, but there aren't many of them. Are you one?

A Mighty Fortress Is Our God
Martin Luther (1483–1546)

A mighty fortress is our God, a bulwark never failing;
Our helper He, amid the flood of mortal ills prevailing:
For still our ancient foe doth seek to work us woe;
His craft and power are great, and, armed with cruel hate,
On earth is not his equal.

Did we in our own strength confide,
Our striving would be losing;
Were not the right Man on our side,
The Man of God's own choosing:
Dost ask who that may be? Christ Jesus, it is He;
Lord Sabaoth, His Name, from age to age the same,
And He must win the battle.

And though this world, with devils filled,
Should threaten to undo us,
We will not fear, for God hath willed
His truth to triumph through us:
The Prince of Darkness grim, we tremble not for him;
His rage we can endure, for lo, his doom is sure,
One little word shall fell him.

That word above all earthly powers,
No thanks to them, abideth;
The Spirit and the gifts are ours
Through Him who with us sideth:
Let goods and kindred go, this mortal life also;
The body they may kill: God's truth abideth still,
His kingdom is forever.

7

BREAKING THE STATIC CONDITION AND GOING ON

Stand fast therefore in the liberty wherewith Christ hath made us free, and be not entangled again with the yoke of bondage.

GALATIANS 5:1

One of the great problems dating back to the Early Church was that of the static Christian. The static Christian is one who is slowed in his spiritual progress. This is a problem we need to face today in the Christian Church. The great challenge is how do we get such Christians interested in becoming more than the average run-of-the-mill type of believers we see everywhere. So many Christians are static or are becoming static in their Christian experience.

The apostle Paul said, "Ye did run well; who did hinder you that ye should not obey the truth?" (Gal. 5:7). So the spiritual progress is stunted, slowed and going nowhere—it is static. Along with this is a lack of moral dynamics, which every Christian ought to know. I believe, if we will listen, we will hear God speaking: "He that hath an ear, let him hear what the Spirit saith unto the churches" (Rev. 2:7). If we could hear what the Spirit is saying today, we would hear Him say:

Moses my servant is dead; now therefore arise, go over this Jordan, thou, and all this people, unto the land which I do give to them, even to the children of Israel. Every place that the sole of your foot shall tread upon, that have I given unto you, as I said unto Moses (Josh. 1:2-3).

I earnestly believe we will hear the Spirit of God say, "Let us go on to perfection." Let us go beyond repentance from past sins, let us get beyond forgiveness and cleansing, let us go beyond the impartation of divine life. Let us first be sure we get these things settled to the point of absolute assurance. No deeper life can exist until life has first been established. No progress can be made in the way until we are in the way. No growth can happen until there has been new birth. All the efforts toward a deeper life, the crucified life, will only bring disappointment unless we have settled the matters of repentance from dead works, the forgiveness of sins and the impartation of divine light and conversion.

I want to break down for you two rather important requirements of the crucified life. These two things will go a long way in breaking the static condition. First, living the crucified life involves completely forsaking the world. Second, the crucified life means turning fully to the Lord Jesus Christ. This is the emphasis of the Bible in both the Old and New Testaments and is the standard formula that has come down to us from the very early days of the Church. You will find it written into the great hymns of the Church and the great books of devotion down through the years. These two things are necessary for a Christian who wants to go on and break the static condition of his life and become a growing, moving, progressive, dynamic Christian.

Completely Forsake the World

It is entirely possible to be religious, go to church every Sunday and yet not to have forsaken the world at all. The proof is that you will find professed Christians wherever you will find non-Christians. I want to be as broad-minded and fair as I can about this. I suppose there are places where you will not find a man claiming to be Christian. I do not know whether criminals who habitually destroy those who are their rivals—taking them out and shooting them—I do not know whether you find any professed Christians among them or not. I do know, however, that when certain criminals have died—by the bullet or whatever means—they have been heard to mumble something about their faith in God, and I suppose they think they have been escorted into the kingdom of God. Some people, though, try very hard to get these bloody men into the kingdom of God, unsaved, unblessed, unshriven, unforgiven. Men who don't even have the time to say, "God have mercy on me as a sinner." People try to get them into heaven simply by performing a religious service or by saying the criminal was a member of some religion or another.

I remember a young man who was a murderer had been sentenced to die in the electric chair in the Cook County Jail. His death had been set for certain day, but the date was changed because the original date fell on a holiday of his religion. They did not want to put him to death on a holy day of his religion. So they changed the day of his death to honor his religious holiday.

So you will find Christians—or those who claim they are Christians—just about everywhere. There has never been a sport invented so violent and vicious that you will not find Christians sitting around watching it with a New Testament in their hip pocket. I do not think there is any worldly pleasure anywhere that you will not find a Christian partaking of it. It is possible to be religious and not forsake the world. It is possible to forsake the world in body yet never forsake it in spirit. It is possible to forsake the world externally and still be worldly inside. Yet nobody can be a Christian in the right sense of the word until he has forsaken the world.

Isolated Nuns

The situation among nuns has been exactly that—forsaking the world and fully turning to Christ—but not among them all. I do not say this because I am a Protestant but because I have read what they have had to say about themselves. Great Christian souls tried to reform nuns in the thirteenth century and get them to be in their inner life what they were in their external outer life. They were hidden away from the world and their bodies were dressed in a certain way in order to show that they were separated from the world. Yet some of these great souls declared that these very people who separated themselves from the world were worldlier than some of those who were not so separated.

Great devotional writers tried hard to rouse the Church of their day that the nuns should be inwardly what their profession showed them to be outwardly. One such writer was Walter Hilton, who lived 200 years before Luther was born, so he never heard of Protestantism or the Reformation. Yet this English Christian was so strong in his faith that he wrote a series of letters to the nuns of a certain convent and warned them of this very thing. That series of letters is called *The Scale of Perfection*. It is a most wonderful book.

The opening chapter of this book is devoted to this subject. Hilton challenges the sisters to live on the inside what they appear to be like on the outside. In essence, he says, "You have come out of the world and closed the door on yourself and put on a certain garb, which indicates you are separated from the world. Now look out that you do not take the world with you into the nunnery and be as worldly in there as you were out on the street. Remember that it is the forsaking of the world in your heart that makes you unworldly."

Hilton urgently warns that it is entirely possible to put on the garb of the nun, live in a nunnery and still be worldly inside. It is possible to be religious and not forsake the world, and it is possible to forsake the world in body but not in spirit. It is never possible, however, to forsake the world in spirit if it is not forsaken in practice.

Shaky Sanctification

It is necessary to mention this because some supposed broad-minded Christians would do almost anything that anybody will do. I have noticed that all you have to do is add "for God" or "for Jesus" onto a thing and, lo and behold, that which the Church has repudiated and earnest Christians have for years forsaken suddenly becomes sanctified. "I'm doing it for God." "I'm doing it for Jesus."

If you just get those prepositional phrases in at the end, something that was not ever counted right by the Church down through the generations, it is now suddenly looked on as right. This attitude takes in almost everything that the world has ever done. I am expecting one of these days to hear about the Association of Christian Bartenders who are "doing it for Jesus." "Oh, we're not like the world. We're not serving up this poison just in our own name. Before we accepted Christ, we used to deal this out for our sakes and for the money we made out of it, but now we're doing it for Jesus." The situation has not gotten that far yet, but give it time—we are on the way. All we have to do is wait a little, and we will sanctify almost anything by saying we do it for Jesus.

I warn you that you cannot do anything for Jesus that Jesus would not do. You cannot do anything for God that God has forbidden and turned the canon of judgments against. The only thing I can do for God is that which is holy like God, and the only thing that I can do for Jesus is that which Jesus has allowed and permitted and commanded me to do. But to live like the world and say, "I'm separated from the world in spirit, and I don't have to separate from the world because I'm separated in spirit" is contradictory. I know where this idea came from. If you sniff a little, you know what you smell? Brimstone. Because that statement comes from hell and certainly belongs there and does not belong in the Church of Christ. It is never possible to forsake the world in your spirit and not forsake it in reality. Let me illustrate what I mean.

Some Biblical Examples

Look at Noah. God said to Noah, "I'm going to destroy the world. Make me an ark; make it out of gopher wood" (see Gen. 6:13-14). Noah obeyed.

Now just suppose I had preached on separation from the world and said to Noah, "Noah, don't you think you ought to get into the ark?"

"Why," Noah would say, "that's the old-fashioned idea. After all, what is the world?"

The modern Church cannot agree on what is meant by "the world." According to modern teaching, "I am separated from the world in my heart, but I am going to stay right down here on the ground and sleep under the bushes and eat off the tree and live like other people. But I won't be of the world because I'm separated in my heart."

What would have happened to Noah if he had had that attitude? Before long he would have been sending up bubbles when the fountains of the great deep broke, the rain came down and the flood covered the mountaintops. Noah's body would have floated and descended along with the rest. However, Noah knew that to forsake the world meant to forsake the world. The Bible says he went into the ark, and God closed the door (see Gen. 7:16).

Now look at Abraham. God said, "Abram, get thee out of thy country, and from thy kindred . . . unto a land that I will shew thee" (Gen. 12:1). Abraham could have said, "I've had a call from God to forsake my country and my people and go to another land. But I do not think I should take that literally. I think that means forsake in spirit, so I'm going to live right here in Ur of the Chaldeans, and I'm going to go into the Holy Land in spirit."

Ridiculous. Abraham had to get out of the country in fact, so he departed, with Lot and his family. He had to forsake one thing in order to enter into the other.

Take *Lot* as another example. Lot finally got to Sodom and became an official of the town. The angels came to him and said, "Escape for thy life; look not behind thee" (Gen. 19:17).

Lot could have said, "Let's have a panel discussion on 'escape for thy life, look not behind thee.' What does it mean?" While engaged in discussing and debating the issue, the fire would have fallen and destroyed Sodom and Lot along with the rest. But Lot knew that "escape for thy life" meant get out of Sodom and stay out, for fire is coming.

The Christian Community

When the Early Christians were told that the love of the world and the things of the world meant they did not love God, they did not hold discussions on what "the world" meant or how far they could go and still please God. They got out of the world; they separated themselves completely from everything that had the world's spirit. The result was that they brought down the world's fury on their own heads.

The world that existed then still exists today. The great God Almighty either now or later will confirm the truth of it, but the world is no different now than it was when they crucified Jesus and martyred the first Christians. It is the same world. Adam is always Adam wherever you find him, and he never changes. The reason we get along with the world so well is that we have compromised our position and allowed it to dictate to us while we in turn are permitted to dictate very little to the world. The result is that very few of us are in any way embarrassed by the world.

What the Church needs to fear is becoming accepted in the community. Any church that the unsaved worldly community accepts is never a church full of the Holy Spirit. Any church that is full of the Holy Spirit, separated from the world and walking with God, will never be accepted by any worldly community. It will always be looked on as being somewhat out of the ordinary. The laws might be set to protect us, and civilization might be such that Christians will not be physically attacked, but crucified Christians will be looked on as being a little bit off-center from what is considered the norm.

Someone once suggested that every Christian should get into a spacesuit, zoom out of here and get as far away from the world as possible. I am not saying that at all. I *am* saying that there is a world that is not the world God means when He said, "Love not [forsake] the world." You need to work and live and drink and sleep and bathe and grow and beget your kind and bring your children up in the world God made. That is not the world I am referring to.

The world we are to forsake is the one that organizes and fills itself with unbelief. The world that passes to amuse itself and build itself upon doubts, unbelief and self-righteousness. Jesus was in the world but not of the world. There is no contradiction here in what I am saying. There is a distinction between that part of the world that is divinely given, where Christians plant, reap, sow, work and live in the world by following God's commandments. God meant it to be so, and that is not "worldliness." Worldliness is the pride of life and the desire for what the eye sees and the longing of the ambitious soul for position and all that which the world does because of the sin in it. This includes all that is the world that overflows into a thousand things the Church has traditionally rejected.

Turn Wholly to the Lord Jesus Christ

So, the first step is to forsake completely the world, which is all negative, and turn your back on it. In so doing, you turn wholly to the Lord Jesus Christ, which is all positive. It is impossible to have a positive without a negative. The battery in your automobile is both positive and negative. If it were 100 percent positive, it wouldn't work. And if it were 100 percent negative, it wouldn't work either. There must be a balance of both positive and negative.

There are those who want to preach all positives, but positives without negatives do not exist. There are also those who want to preach only negatives, a list of all the things you cannot do. But you cannot have love without hate. You cannot have light without darkness. The one follows the other.

If I am to wholly follow the Lord Jesus Christ, I must forsake everything that is contrary to Him. The following is contingent on the forsaking. The positive must be balanced by the negative.

It is this that defines living the crucified life, not the turning away. That is negative. You can forsake the world, quit gambling, quit drinking, quit smoking, quit living for the world, stop going to any of the worldly places of amusement, quit dancing, never do any of these things. You can quit all that is negative and has no power to impart any life of any kind. But these negatives are necessary before there can be the positive.

The positive is that you turn to Jesus Christ. That is what gives the power and authority and the deep satisfaction of "joy unspeakable and full of glory" (1 Pet. 1:8). The negative can never shine. The negative can never be musical. The negative can never be fragrant. A man can go live in a cave, leaving everything behind in utter disgust, like time in a vacuum. He can escape into the woods, live in a cave and still not have any power, any radiance of joy, any inward glory. It is only turning to Jesus Christ that does this. And the two can be done in one act. If I am facing north and God commands me to turn south, I can do that in one easy motion. So when God says to forsake the world and turn to Christ, that can be done in one motion, one free and easy act. My turning from the world *is* my turning to Christ. It does not always work that way, but it can.

Suppose someone who had great power decided to do something about the darkness. Suppose this someone had a lot of gremlins or angels or something at his command and said, "I'm tired of this darkness. I want you to wipe the heavens clean of darkness." Suppose he got a thousand or a million or 10 million gremlins (or some other kind of imaginary beings) with mops and the creatures mopped the heavens of all the darkness. It would still be dark. Just wait until the sun comes up. The coming up of the sun will do what all the mopping of the heavens can never do. Just wait for the sun, that's all.

Imagine a young man who will not drink soda pop because it is worldly. So he sits at a soda counter and is disturbed about a glass of soda in front of him and complains that he feels a little worldly. Well, he is simply an unhappy man. I have never seen a happy Christian yet who was the least bit conscious of or concerned about the world. Never.

I have also never seen a happy Christian yet who was not taken up with Jesus Christ the Lord. The sun comes up, and the darkness goes out. No creature in the universe can wipe the heavens clean of the darkness; only the sun can do that. When the sun peeks out in the morning, it parts the darkness and the clouds flee away and the shadows are no more.

So when we turn with all our hearts to Jesus Christ our Lord, we find the deeper life, the crucified life. We find in Him the power to mature and the satisfaction and "joy unspeakable and full of glory." When we turn our eyes to gaze on the Son of God and our hearts are taken up with His person, every instrument inside our musical hearts beats, and the music starts. Then the radiance breaks out and, as Peter said, "ye rejoice with joy unspeakable and full of glory."

This is what I mean by turning to the crucified life. These two acts can be done at once. Turn from the world and turn to Christ. And all the natural things like eating, drinking, buying, selling, marrying—all the things that God created to be done that are not of the spirit of the world but are natural and of God—will all be sanctified. They will become fuel for the fires of the altar of God. So the common things, things that we call secular, will no longer be secular to us. The mundane things will be mundane no more, but heavenly. The most common thing can be done for the glory of God when we have turned from the world and the world's ways and look into the full face of the Son of God. The sun will shine and not all the gremlins of hell can wipe the sunlight away.

Hell could send up a legion of gremlins to wipe away the sunshine, and they could desperately follow the sun around the earth and never succeed in keeping the sunshine away from the earth, because when the sun shines on the earth, there *will be* sunshine. So hell cannot destroy earth or disrupt the spiritual happiness of your gaze into the face of Jesus. We are as free as the Son of righteousness "with healing in his wings" (Mal. 4:2).

Will you turn from the world and turn fully to Christ? This will go a long way in breaking forever the condition of being a static Christian.

Fully Surrendered—Lord, I Would Be
Alfred C. Snead (1884–1961)

Fully surrendered—Lord, I would be,
Fully surrendered, dear Lord, to Thee.
All on the altar laid, surrender fully made,
Thou hast my ransom paid; I yield to Thee.

Fully surrendered—life, time, and all,
All Thou hast given me held at Thy call.
Speak but the word to me, gladly I'll follow Thee,
Now and eternally obey my Lord.

Fully surrendered—silver and gold,
His, who hath given me riches untold.
All, all belong to Thee, for Thou didst purchase me,
Thine evermore to be, Jesus, my Lord.

Fully surrendered—Lord, I am Thine;
Fully surrendered, Savior divine!
Live Thou Thy life in me; all fullness dwells in Thee;
Not I, but Christ in me, Christ all in all.

8

THE GREAT OBSTACLE TO LIVING THE CRUCIFIED LIFE

Trust in the LORD with all thine heart; and lean not unto thine own understanding. In all thy ways acknowledge him, and he shall direct thy paths.

PROVERBS 3:5-6

Paul was a man who knew what he believed and where he stood. He knew God and was confident with a great cosmic confidence, yet that same man was the most distrustful of himself. As great as Paul was, he did not trust himself.

Before man, Paul was as bold as a lion; but before God, Paul could not say too much against himself. When he was in front of God, Paul actually had no confidence in himself at all. His confidence with God was in reverse proportion to his confidence in himself. The amount of self-trust Paul had was as little as the trust he had in God was great.

What do I mean by "self-trust"? Simply, it is the respectability and self-assurance that comes through education. It is what you learn about yourself and what your friends tell you about yourself and all the best that you may give yourself. Self-trust is the last great obstacle to living the crucified life, which is why we mill around the deep river of God like animals around a waterhole, afraid to go in because the water may be too deep. We never quite get it.

I want to quote a little from a man who had a wonderful name: Lorenzo Scupoli (1530–1610). He was one of those strange Catholics who, during his lifetime, was considered more or less a heretic because of his evangelical leaning.

He wrote a book called *The Spiritual Combat*, which is a practical manual for living. Scupoli begins by teaching that the essence of life is continually fighting against our egoistic longings. Scupoli says the way to win the fight is to replace our desires for self-gratification with acts of charity and sacrifice. The one who does not do this loses and suffers eternity in hell. The one who does it, trusting not in his own strength but in God's power, triumphs and will be happy in heaven.

Scupoli analyzes several common, real-life situations and advises on how to cope with each of them to keep your conscience clear and to improve your virtue. Anyone who continues to act against God is the cause of all that is bad. All good comes from God, whose goodness is limitless. Scupoli wrote:

> So necessary is self-distrust in this conflict, that without it you will be unable, I say not to achieve the victory desired, but even to overcome the very least of your passions. Let this be well impressed upon your mind; for our corrupt nature too easily inclines us to a false estimate of ourselves; so that, being really nothing, we account ourselves to be something, and presume, without the slightest foundation, upon our own strength.
>
> This is a fault not easily discerned by us, but very displeasing in the sight of God. For He desires and loves to see in us a frank and true recognition of this most certain truth, that all the virtue and grace which is within us is derived from Him alone, Who is the fountain of all good, and that nothing good can proceed

from us, no, not even a thought which can find accept-
ance in His sight.[1]

Why is self-trust so wrong? Self-trust is wrong because it
robs God. God says, "Will a man rob God? Yet ye have robbed
me. But ye say, Wherein have we robbed thee? In tithes and of-
ferings" (Mal. 3:8). We have robbed God and taken away from
Him what belongs to Him. Paul states that God is the fountain
of all, and nothing, not even good thoughts, can come from us
unless they come from God first (see Rom. 11:35-36). If you ignore the fact that God is the source of everything and make a
converted and sanctified self the source, it is just as bad as it
can be because final trust in God has been taken away. Self
judges God and man and holds God to be less than He is and
man to be more than he is. This is our trouble.

Study theology and learn about how God is the source and
fountain of all things. Learn about the attributes of God and
see if yet in your heart you still believe that God is less than He
is and you are more than you are. Think of the moon. If the
moon could talk like a man and have a personality, it could say
within itself, *I shine on the earth and every time I'm around, the earth
becomes beautiful.* If someone could respond to the moon, they
would say, "Listen, you don't do that by yourself. Don't you
know that you have been discovered and found out? You don't
shine at all. You are simply reflecting the sun's light, so it's
really the sun that shines."

Then self comes to the rescue of the moon. "You're letting
your light shine and you're doing a good job," it says. "When
you're not up, one whole side of the earth lies in darkness. But
when you come up, a side lights up and I can begin to see rows
of houses. You're doing a fine job." The moon would not say,
"The glory belongs to God, because it is only by the grace of

God that I'm like this." All the time the moon is thinking that he is shining.

When the moon is shining, it is only a reflection light from the sun. And if the moon really understood, he could boldly shine and talk about it, because he would know that he was not shining at all. Similarly, Paul knew that he did not have a thing of himself that was fit for heaven. He had only the grace of God in him. It was God and not him. He completely and radically distrusted himself. No man can really know himself; he is not capable of knowing how he feels.

Everybody thinks they know what they sound like until they hear themselves on a recording. One of the most humbling things that ever happened to me was when I had a sermon recorded. For the first time I heard the sound of my own voice, and that recording did not lie to me. Up to that time, I had been told I had a fine preaching voice. Then I heard myself, and nobody needs to talk to me about *that* anymore. I have listened to myself, and I know how I sound. No man knows the sound of his own voice until he hears it, and no man knows how weak he is until God exposes him and nobody wants to be exposed.

It is important that we understand how dangerous it is to trust our good habits and virtues. Only God can bring us to the point of understanding that our strength is indeed our weakness. Anything that we rely on or trust can be our undoing. We do not realize how weak we are until the Holy Spirit begins exposing these things to us.

Dealing with Self-Trust

The question I must pose is simply, how do we learn this self-distrust? Basically, God uses four different ways to deal with this matter. These are supported and confirmed by the devotional writers, the great hymnists and the Christian biographers.

They weave like a common thread through the lives of those who are committed to living the crucified life.

A Flash of Holy Inspiration in Your Soul

I believe the first and best way to deal with self-trust is for God to flash some holy inspiration into your soul and expose it. This has happened to many people. For example, it happened to Brother Lawrence. In *The Practice of the Presence of God,* he wrote that for 40 years he was never once out of the conscious presence of God: "When I took the cross and decided to obey Jesus and walk this holy way, I gathered that I would have to suffer a lot." Then he said something rather strange: "For some reason God never found me worthy of much suffering. He just let me continue to trust Him and I put all my self trust away and I have been trusting in God completely." Brother Lawrence was living the crucified life, believing Christ was in him, around him and near him. And he was praying all the time.

God flashed some holy inspiration into the heart of Lady Julian of Norwich, and because of the revelations she received, she knew instantly that she was no good and that Jesus Christ was everything. She stayed in that position until she died. I think this is probably the easiest way for us to get it—for the Lord to give us a sweet, sudden burst of holy inspiration within our hearts that shows us the real self. Of course, this is where our doctrine gets in our way. We can believe the whole counsel of God, and our life may still be plagued with pride to such an extent that it hides the face of God. It is such pride that prevents us from going forward in victory. This cannot be corrected by a lecture on correct doctrine. Rather, we need the Holy Spirit to tell us the true condition of our soul. We need Him to reveal to us how bad we really are and lead us out of our spiritual swamp.

God-Imposed Physical Discipline

Another way in which God deals with our self-trust is the physical realm. Many people have a hard time believing that God would actually bring physical harm to our bodies. Yet the Scriptures bear out the fact that physical pain is one of God's effective means of dealing with an undisciplined self.

The Old Testament is filled with examples of physical suffering imposed by God, but probably Job stands out above all the rest. A casual reading of Job's story may not get to the real problem that Job had. Certainly, he was a good man, and the Scriptures bear this out. The problem with Job was that he was a good man and he knew it. If you are good but you do not know it, then God can use you. However, if you know how good and great you are, you cease to be a vehicle through which God can send His blessing.

The only way God could get to the center of Job's problem was through physical pain. Sometimes this is the only way He can get our attention. God is not above using this method to deal with the problems of pride and self-trust. And the suffering God sends will sometimes not be curable by any medicine. Of course, the only cure for such a physical ailment is renouncing the self and humbling ourselves before God.

Nobody likes to talk about this sort of thing today. Everybody wants to hear happy, cheerful inspirational thoughts that make us feel good. This is why to get a crowd to come to church today, we need a cowbell, a musical saw or a talking horse to have some fun and a little bit of entertainment for those who are bored with the simple, plain word of God. Nobody wants to hear about physical discipline or pain. After all, we believe in healing.

Extreme Trials and Temptations

Another method God uses to develop distrust of ourselves is extreme trials and temptations. From listening to some preachers and reading some books, it is easy to conclude that once a person is born again, that is the end of it—no more trials or temptations. Those who believe in the infilling of the Holy Spirit have somehow also communicated the idea that this is the end of all Christian experience. But the Bible tells us that after Jesus was filled with the Spirit, He was driven into the wilderness for some severe temptations.

When a Christian faces a difficult or extreme trial or temptation, he is tempted to throw in the towel and say, "God, it's no use. I'm just no good. You obviously don't want me, so I'm finished." All the while he forgets that God wants to teach us through these trials and temptations that self-trust is dangerous and unreliable. At times, when something blows up in our face, we think it is all over instead of taking it as proof that we are not mature Christians. We need to take the blowup as proof that we are nearer to our forever home today than we were yesterday. We need to understand that our heavenly Father is letting these things happen to us to wean us away from trusting ourselves and to move us to lean exclusively on the Lord Jesus Christ.

Some have the idea that repentance is to be a drawn-out affair that includes beating yourself down. I think we need to start with repentance, but there comes a time when we need to just turn everything over to God and then not do it anymore. That is the best repentance in the world. If you did something last week you are ashamed of, feel conviction and condemnation about it, simply say, "I repent." Turn it over to the Lord, tell Him about it, and then do not do it anymore.

What is the purpose of these severe trials and temptations that sometimes cause you to fail? It is not to show you that you are not a true Christian. Rather, it is to show you that your conscience is tender and you are very near to God. The Lord is trying to teach you that last lesson so that you rid yourself of self-distrust. The closer you are to God, the more tender your conscience is before the Lord, and the more severe your trial and temptation may be. Some in the Church have lied to us by inferring that the Christian life is void of difficulty, problems and trials. The exact opposite is the truth.

The great characters of the Bible shed some light on the subject. Remember Jacob's temptation? Remember Peter's temptation? All throughout Scripture (and all of Church history), there are countless individuals who encountered great trials and temptations. Hebrews 11 tells about many of those heroes of faith—those who endured extreme trials and temptations in life.

Sometimes a trial comes along, and we run to the Bible, pull out a quote and say, "According to this Scripture right here, we got it." We have certain confidence in ourselves. We think we know exactly what is going on. The problem is that we do *not* know what is happening, and so God will deal with our self-trust.

God certainly knows our feelings. He knows we are so proud of the way we rightly divide the word of truth and that we can disjoint a text like a butcher getting a chicken ready for the barbecue. With words all carefully laid out and knowing just where to put your finger on this or just where to put your finger on that, you are too smart for God to bless you. You know too much. You can identify everything, but the dear heavenly Father knows you do not really know much at all. He lets things happen to you until you recognize that you do not know what is happening. Your friends do not know what is going on either. And when you go to somebody you feel you can trust, that person will not be able to help you either. That is actually good news.

It truly would be terrible if we had some holy Saint Francis to whom we all could go to find out where we were, what was happening to us and what life is all about. God loves us too much for that. He is trying to teach us to trust Him, not people—to lean on

Him, not on people. I have been so scared that people would start trusting in me and leaning on me. However, fear not! God pulls the crutches out from under me occasionally, just to see if He can trust me.

As a Christian, you know some of the means God uses to teach His people. As a Christian, you love God, but you are sick of all the nonsense in the world. You are sick of all the nonsense in the Church. Your heart is crying after God just as the doe yearns after the water brooks. Your heart and your flesh cry out for the living God. Yet in spite of all this, you still trust yourself. You testify that you love your Bible and that your time of prayer is precious, but still your tendency is to trust yourself.

This tendency is more difficult to deal with because we do not talk about this anymore. This teaching left the evangelical and fundamental church a generation ago. Nowadays when someone becomes a Christian, everybody slaps him on the back and says, "Glory to God, Brother, you are born again!"

Ah, but the Lord says, "That's only the beginning." The Scriptures teach that God will rejoice over us with joy and with singing. This is not a picture of an angry God. Rather, it is a picture of a loving Father who is everlastingly patient toward us, His children. God is not judging us. God only wants His children to grow and develop into full-fledged Christians. Sometimes in order to accomplish this, God must send us through severe and harsh trials and temptations. But the destination is Christian perfection in the person of the Lord Jesus Christ.

The Footprints of the Age-Old Saints
I would condense the fourth thing God uses in dealing with our self-trust into one simple thought: Look around for the saintly footprints where you are right now. You are not alone in this journey. Look around for footprints and find out who

made those footprints. You will notice that the footprints are those of the great saints who lived in ages past.

I am not interested in any of the modern footprints. I am interested only in those footprints that have come to us down through the centuries. If you look around and see these footprints, you will find them all going in the same direction. You will find they follow the footprints of Jesus. They are all going in the same direction. Look carefully and you will see some of them backtracking a little occasionally, but you will also see that they found their way at last and went back to following after Jesus. They are all following Christ.

Trust God

Now, the absolutely cheerful and confident Christian can expect this very same thing. You want the Lord to do something for you, don't you? You want Him to come down on you with a wave of grace. As a congregation, we want to again see the Reformation or a revival coming down on us with power. We want to see power in our individual lives. We want the Holy Spirit to come on us and demonstrate His power. We want to see all of that, but we need to be careful that we're not trying to work it up on our own.

I do not intend to try to work up anything. You cannot climb Jacob's ladder without sweat, perspiration and hard work. The work of God is not dependent on any man's schedule. I rarely know where I am going in my life's journey, but after I have been there a year, I can look back and see that my path has been relatively straight. I go to God, write out my prayers, wait on Him and remind Him, but nothing seems to happen. I seem to be getting nowhere, and then suddenly things break around me. I look back and see that God has been leading my every step, and I did not even know it.

I did not know where I was going, but looking back, I can see where I have been. I do not think we should always look back, but at least we should be able to look back and see the terrain where God has led us—the valleys and plateaus He has brought us through because He loves us in spite of ourselves.

The more my trust rests in God, the less I trust myself. If we truly desire to live the crucified life, we must get rid of self-trust and trust only in God.

We Give Thee but Thine Own
William W. How (1823–1897)

We give thee but Thine own,
Whate'er the gift may be;
All that we have is Thine alone,
A trust, O Lord, from Thee.

May we Thy bounties thus
As stewards true receive,
And gladly, as Thou blessest us,
To Thee our firstfruits give.

O hearts are bruised and dead,
And homes are bare and cold,
And lambs for whom the Shepherd bled
Are straying from the fold.

To comfort and to bless,
To find a balm for woe,
To tend the lone and fatherless
Is angels' work below.

The captive to release,
To God the lost to bring,
To teach the way of life and peace
It is a Christ-like thing.

And we believe Thy Word,
Though dim our faith may be;
Whate'er for Thine we do, O Lord,
We do it unto Thee.

Note

1. Father Dom Lorenzo Scupoli, *The Spiritual Combat,* chapter 8. http://www.holyro
   mancatholicchurch.org/articles/SpiritualCombat.htm.

PART III

. . . .

THE PERILS
OF THE
CRUCIFIED
LIFE

9

THE CURRENCY OF THE CRUCIFIED LIFE

What things were gain to me, those I counted loss for Christ.
Yea doubtless, and I count all things but loss for the excellency of the
knowledge of Christ Jesus my Lord: for whom I have suffered the loss
of all things, and do count them but dung, that I may win Christ.

PHILIPPIANS 3:7-8

When God calls a man to follow Him, He calls that man to follow Him regardless of the cost. The enemy can do his worst, but if a man is in God's hands, no harm can come to him. Nobody asked what it would cost a person to become a great football player. Or what it would cost a person to become a successful attorney. Or what it would cost a person to become a successful businessman. Everybody knows that the more important something is, the higher the cost. What costs you little or nothing is worth exactly that much. The challenge before us is simply this: What are we willing to pay, sacrifice or surrender in order to advance in living the crucified life?

Church history and Christian biography are filled with examples of what people have been willing to pay to live the crucified life. The martyrs of the Church form a long and glorious line. From the standpoint of the natural world, this sort of life does not look glamorous. But when we look at it from God's point of view, it takes on an altogether different perspective. The first Christian martyr was Stephen, who died at the feet of Saul, who later became the great apostle Paul. I am quite sure that Stephen's death made a great impression upon the young Saul.

That there has been over the last half a century a steady decline in the spiritual quality of Christian religion in America, no informed person will attempt to deny. I am not speaking of liberalism or modernism but of that evangelical wing of Christianity to which I myself belong by theological conviction and personal choice. I believe the situation has become so serious that the earnest observer is forced to wonder whether our popular evangelical religion today is indeed the true faith of our fathers or simply some form of paganism thinly disguised with a veneer of Christianity to make it acceptable to those who want to call themselves Christian.

Turn to the church page of any city newspaper or leaf through some of the popular magazines today and what you find there will make you sick at heart. We have come to our present low state as the result of an almost fanatical emphasis on grace to the total exclusion of obedience, self-discipline, patience, personal holiness, cross carrying, discipleship and other such precious doctrines of the New Testament. These doctrines cannot be made to harmonize with the doctrine of grace as taught by most modern Church fathers. Certainly, though these teachings are not denied, they are either allowed to die from neglect or relegated to a footnote with so many explanations and interpretations as to make them ineffective.

The grace that amazed our fathers—that brought them to their knees in tears and trembling worship—has by deadly familiarity become so mundane that it scarcely affects us at all. That which was so wondrously precious to the Moravians and Methodists and their immediate spiritual descendents has become cheap to a generation of Christians devoted to their own pursuits and engrossed in their own pleasures.

Dietrich Bonhoeffer

In my mind, one man epitomizes what one must pay, or give up, for the crucified life. That man was Dietrich Bonhoeffer, who lived under the shadow of the mad nihilist Adolf Hitler.

Bonhoeffer was in his thirties when the Nazis came to power. He was a brilliant scholar, theologian and a leader in the confessional church in Germany, and his keen, perceptive mind told him that the political consequences of national socialism would be a bloody war for Germany and the world. His sensitive Christian heart recoiled from the unbelievable malignity of Hitler and his band of assassins. As a preacher of the gospel, Bonhoeffer went boldly to the airwaves and warned his nation of the inevitable consequences of a political system "which corrupted and grossly misled the nation that made the 'Fuhrer' its idol and God."[1]

As the war clouds formed over Europe, Bonhoeffer left Germany and carried on his work in England. It was not long before his Christian conscience would not allow him to be in a place of safety when his country was experiencing turmoil:

> "I shall have no right to participate in the reconstruction of Germany after the war," he said, "if I do not share the trials of this time with my people. . . . Christians in Germany will face the terrible alternative of either willing the defeat of their nation in order that Christian civilization may survive, or willing the victory of their nation and thereby destroying our civilization. I know which of these alternatives I must choose; but I cannot make this choice in security."[2]

After returning to Germany, Bonhoeffer worked for the confessional church and with the political underground. He was soon arrested by the infamous Gestapo and clapped into jail, along with other members of his family. From then on, he was shuttled to different prisons and to different concentration camps. During this time, he served his fellow prisoners by witnessing, praying, comforting and assisting in every way possible. Those who knew him at the time tell of his "calmness and self-control . . . even in the most terrible situations." He was, they said, "a giant before man . . . but a child before God."[3]

Bonhoeffer was the German Luther, a man of remarkable spiritual insight. He did all he could to preach Jesus Christ as the Savior of man and embraced what he called "costly grace." He said that we shouldn't try to get into heaven cheaply, for the grace of God would cost us everything we have. The grace of God is costly because it cost Christ His blood, and it will cost us everything—maybe even our lives.

At the beginning of the war, Bonhoeffer was engaged to a lovely young woman. His sister, father and other relatives were also still living at the time. The Nazis pulled the old totalitarian trick: "You better buckle down and shut up, because we've got your family as hostages. And if you don't do what we ask you to do, it's your family who will suffer." That was their technique, so they told Bonhoeffer, "You surrender and shut up about costly grace and freedom in the gospel of Jesus Christ. Stop warning against Hitler and the Nazis, or we will kill your family."

Those sorts of threats usually work, but the Nazis had never come up against a man like Dietrich Bonhoeffer. With a calmness and serenity that only Christ can give, Bonhoeffer replied, "My family belongs to God, and you'll never get me to surrender by threatening to kill my family."

Years before, Bonhoeffer had written, "When God calls a man, he bids him come and die."[4] On April 9, 1945, at the Flossenbürg concentration camp, Bonhoeffer was called on to do just that. He refused to allow himself to be rescued, lest he endanger the lives of certain others, so "he went steadfastly on his way to be hanged, and died with admirable calmness and dignity."[5]

Too many of the German people had grown arrogant with national pride and dangerously bloated with temporary success. So God in His mercy sent His man—a seeing man—to the country of the blind. But the nation of blind men hanged their prophet, cremated his body and scattered his ashes. It was only shortly after this that the blind men themselves faced national humiliation and final collapse.

No doubt, the greatest contribution of Bonhoeffer's ministry is his book *The Cost of Discipleship*. Even before the war, this prophet saw clearly. He wrote, "Cheap grace is the deadly enemy of our Church. We are fighting today for costly grace."[6]

Only the knowledge that truth is universal and that mankind is very much the same the world over enables us to understand how this young Lutheran minister, examining German Christianity in the mid-1930s, could diagnose so skillfully the disease that threatens to destroy evangelicalism in America a generation later. What concerns me is that what Bonhoeffer said of conditions in Germany then is terribly, frighteningly true of American Christianity today. The parallel is alarming.

Worldly Legs

Why do God's people not bounce right out and start going, rising, mounting, soaring and climbing? Why do they have to be petted, cuddled, looked after, followed around and held up? The reason is that they never acquired spiritual legs under them and the face of God is turned away from them. That is, they think that is the case; the truth is that Christ made full atonement for us so there is nothing between a Christian and God. Christ's atonement was so perfect and complete that it turns all that is against us into something that is for us. It turned all our demerits into merits. It moved everything that was on the debit side of the ledger to the credit side of the ledger. Everything that was against us was moved over to our side. That is the wonder of the atonement in Jesus Christ.

So why is it that we take so long to rid ourselves of this veil of obscurity? Why do we take so long to push it aside, see the sun shining and make our way up to the peak of our faith?

It is not God's fault, because floundering is not God's will for us. God wills that His children should grow in grace and in the knowledge of Jesus Christ. He wills that we should go on to perfection. He wills that we should be holy. So why don't we strive to be holy? The major problem is that we like ourselves too much. We struggle to keep up a good front.

A Good Front

I've seen some pity-seekers come to the altar, but as a rule, I do not pity them because they are struggling. Some might say, "Look at that. Isn't that wonderful?" But I say, "You know why they are struggling? They are fighting God." That is never a good sight to see. They are trying to keep up a good front, they do not want to surrender, they do not want people to know how unimportant they are and how useless and how small. They do not want anyone to peek into the poverty of their hearts. So they struggle to keep up a good front.

Americans spend billions of dollars yearly just to keep up a good front. Tear the front down of the average person and you will find he is a poor tramp in his spirit, in his mind and in his heart. We try to hide that inward state, disguise our poverty and preserve our reputation to keep some authority for ourselves. We want to have a little authority in the world. We do not want to give it all up. But God wants to take all authority out of our hands and get us to the place where we have no authority left at all. He wants to take it all away, and He will never bless us until He has taken it all away. As long as you are in command, as long as you say, "Now listen, God, I'll tell you how to do this," you will only be a mediocre Christian, dull of hearing, attending camp meetings, churches and having all the means of grace at your disposal, but still getting nowhere.

We like to have a little glory for ourselves. We are willing to let God have most of it, but we want a commission, just a little bit for ourselves. We want to rescue part of ourselves from the cost.

I am inclined to think that some people were just born to be little. They never amount to much. If they go to heaven, it will be by the grace of God, and they will take nothing along—they will go empty-handed. They will get through by the mercy of God. That is the only way anybody gets through, but God wills that you should take with you riches, diamonds, pearls, silver and gold tried in the fire. He wills that you should have a harvest of souls. He wills that you should send your good works before you. He wills that you should be a productive, fruitful Christian.

Yet a great many Christians are not going to have a thing to show God. They are simply not willing to pay the price. The writer of Hebrews said, "Ye are dull of hearing" (Heb. 5:11). He could not talk to his readers the way he wanted to, because while they had time enough to grow and mature, they had not.

Self-Defense

The truth is that we must stop defending ourselves, always having our fists clenched a little bit. We had a dear old woman who used to help at the altar. When she saw somebody praying with his fist closed, she would say to him, "Now, open your fist, honey. To pray with your fist closed means you are hanging on to something. Let it go. Let it go. Open your hands for God. That's it."

Whatever holds you back is a veil between you and God, and it is made up of things that are just silly. You will never be more than a common Christian until you give up your own interest and cease defending yourself. Put yourself in the hands of God and let Him alone. Stop trying to help God.

I never had a tooth pulled without trying to help the dentist struggle with the labor. Whenever I travel in an airplane, I instinctively try to help the pilot by leaning to the left and then leaning to the right. We are just as silly as that when it comes to the things of God. We want to help God out. No. Give yourself to God. Turn yourself over to Him and say, "Father, I'm sick of being a common Christian. I am sick of this mediocrity, of being halfway to where I ought to be, of seeing other Christians happy when I am not. I am weary of the whole thing. I want to go on, and I want to know You."

One man had a great experience with God, one that blossomed and grew into an even more wondrous experience. He walked with God and became known as a man of God. People came to him and said, "Brother, you were known for a long time as just average and suddenly you're blessed all over. What happened to you?"

"Well," he said, "I don't rightly know, but here's what happened and how it happened. One day I appeared before God and said, 'God, I have something to say to You. Never as long as I live will I say anything in prayer that I don't mean.' And then from there I started out."

The Currency to Exchange

Most Christians are satisfied living their entire lives as common Christians. They never experience the richness of what it truly means to be a Christian. Without a deep insatiable hunger for the things of God, there is nothing within them prodding them to go forward to perfection. The condition of today's Christian Church is the result of too many common Christians in leadership roles. Once again, we need a great move of the Holy Spirit to break out of the spiritual rut and press on to spiritual perfection. That move needs to start with individual Christians who are willing to give all to God and live the crucified life.

But just what is the currency associated with living the crucified life? What exactly is the currency that must be used in this exchange? Let me enumerate several things that I think we need to exchange in order to move on in our journey through the crucified life.

Safety

One of the first things that we need to exchange is our safety. Those who insist on a safe environment are never going to move forward in their journey to the crucified life. Dietrich Bonheoffer did not have safety in his life. In order for him to do what God wanted him to do, he had to exchange his safety. If safety had been important to him, he never would have gone back to Germany and face what he knew he was going to face. If your safety is so precious that you must preserve it at all costs, you will be hindered on your journey along the crucified-life pathway. Your safety is the price you pay to move on to new spiritual vistas.

Convenience

Another aspect of our currency along this line is convenience. Nobody that I have ever read about ever found dying to be convenient. The journey along the crucified-life pathway will be paid for by "mountains" of inconvenience. Those who are willing to part with their convenience will progress toward being hundredfold Christians.

Fun

Perhaps there has never been a generation of Christians who were more in love with fun than the present one. But this is also part of the currency to pay for the journey to the crucified life. None of the marchers in the Church found it to be fun. The great reformers of the church sacrificed fun in order to do what God had before them. It comes down to this: Hang on to your fun or exchange it for progress toward spiritual perfection.

Popularity

Many today are trying to make Christianity popular by marketing it as if it were a product on a store shelf. Nowhere in my reading of history have I ever discovered that what was popular with the crowd was right. In most instances, in order to move ahead, most great men and women of God had to lean against the wind of popularity. The cost for their advancement was their popularity.

Worldly Success

One more thing I might mention that must be exchanged on this journey is worldly success. Are you willing to exchange your success in business, in sports, in your career, in order to move forward and achieve spiritual perfection?

If we look at success from the world's perspective, Jesus' ministry was a terrible failure. All the apostles failed as far as the world's criterion is concerned. The great martyrs of the Church were absolute failures. According to the criterion of the world's idea of success, William Tyndale, who died because of his work, was an absolute failure.

The man or woman who is willing to exchange and surrender all aspects of his or her success is the one who is going to go on with God. We are not living for this world but for the world to come. The economy we are bartering in is not of this world but of the world where Jesus Christ is preparing a place for us. We have the awesome privilege of exchanging worldly success for favor with our Father which art in heaven.

The crucified life is an expensive proposition. Whoever is willing to pay the price is the one who will go forward in absolute victory and joyous fellowship with Christ. Christ paid the price for our salvation; we now pay the price for our full identification with Him and our walk and pilgrimage toward spiritual perfection.

New Year 1945
Dietrich Bonhoeffer (1906–1945)

With every power for good to stay and guide me,
Comforted and inspired beyond all fear,
I'll live these days with You in thought beside me,
And pass, with You, into the coming year.

The old year still torments our hearts, unhastening:
The long days of our sorrow still endure.
Father, grant to the soul Thou hast been chastening
That Thou hast promised—the healing and the cure.

Should it be ours to drain the cup of grieving
Even to the dregs of pain, at Thy command,
We will not falter, thankfully receiving
All that is given by Thy loving hand.

But, should it be Thy will once more to release us
To life's enjoyment and its good sunshine,
That we've learned from sorrow shall increase us
And all our life be dedicate as Thine.

Today, let candles shed their radiant greeting:
Lo, on our darkness are they not Thy light,
Leading us haply to our longed-for meeting?
Thou canst illumine e'en our darkest night.

When now the silence deepens for our harkening,
Grant we may hear Thy children's voices raise
From all the unseen world around us darkening
Their universal paean, in Thy praise.

While all the powers of Good aid and attend us,
Boldly we'll face the future, be it what may.
At even, and at morn, God will befriend us,
And oh, most surely on each new year's day!

Notes

1. G. Leibholz, "Memoir," in Dietrich Bonhoeffer, *The Cost of Discipleship* (New York: Simon and Schuster, 1959), p. 16.
2. Dietrich Bonhoeffer, *The Cost of Discipleship* (New York: Simon and Schuster, 1959), pp. 17-18.
3. Leibholz, "Memoir," in Bonhoeffer, *The Cost of Discipleship*, p. 19.
4. Ibid., p. 11.
5. Ibid., p. 26.
6. Ibid., p. 43.

10

THE VEILS
THAT OBSCURE
GOD'S FACE

Brethren, I count not myself to have apprehended:
but this one thing I do, forgetting those things which are behind, and
reaching forth unto those things which are before, I press toward the
mark for the prize of the high calling of God in Christ Jesus.

PHILIPPIANS 3:13-14

The New Testament message, objectives and methods have been allowed to lie dormant. Acts done in the name of the Lordship of Jesus Christ are Lordship in name only. Replacing Christ's true Lordship, we have introduced our own message, our own objectives and our own methods for achieving those objectives, which are, in every case, not scriptural at all.

Is it heresy—does it constitute a radical mind—if you pray for God to cleanse the intent of your heart with the unspeakable gift of His grace? This, of course, is the great prayer by the author of *The Cloud of Unknowing:* "God . . . I beseech Thee so for to cleanse the intent of mine heart with the unspeakable gift of Thy grace, that I may perfectly love Thee, and worthily praise Thee."

To long to love God and worthily praise Him should mean more than the words you say. It should cost you everything. Is that heresy? Should a man be put in jail for that? Should he be ostracized for it in the light of our hymnody, in the light of our devotional books, in the light of Church history all the way back to Paul and in the light of the lives of all the saints? No, I do not think so.

The apostle Paul said that to gain Christ, he would have renounced this entire world (see Phil. 3:7-8). He wanted everyone to know Christ as a conscious experience, to use the modern phrasing, and to receive the kingdom of heaven. He said that he prayed all the time for Christ to dwell in the heart of every believer (see Eph. 3:17). He told the Corinthians, "Examine yourselves, whether ye be in the faith; prove your own selves. Know ye not your own selves, how that Jesus Christ is in you, except ye be reprobates?" (2 Cor. 13:5). He told the Romans, "Now if a man have not the Spirit of Christ, he is none of his" (Rom. 8:9). It is by the indwelling of Jesus that we receive the riches of God and see His smiling face.

Unfortunately, there has developed between the Christian and the face of God what I will call "veils of obscurity." These veils hide the precious riches of God from those of us who press on to perfection. The effect is that we can no longer see the smiling face of God.

Recognize the Veils

On a dark cloudy day, the brightness of the sun is obscured. The sun is still there, but our ability to benefit from the sun's rays is greatly reduced. So it is in the spiritual world. There are certain veils that come between us and God and have a similar effect. These veils are usually of our own making. We allow them to develop in our lives, and most of the time we are not even aware of the total impact they are having on us. Let me describe some of the veils that are the most troubling.

Pride and Stubbornness

No doubt the first and strongest of these veils are pride and stubbornness. Nothing is more Adamic in our lives than these. The root of both of these is an inflated opinion of our own selves. That which causes us the most problem is that which we honor the most.

One term often used in this regard is the word "ego." This one word conveys the root of all of our problems with ourselves, with our families, with our friends and certainly with our God. It is when we usurp God's rightful place that the trouble occurs. The reason we do that is because we think more highly of ourselves than anybody else, including God.

Even if we find ourselves to be wrong, stubbornness will prohibit us from acknowledging that fact, so we cannot press forward. The problem with pride and stubbornness is that they focus on us and obscure the face of God, the One who in all cases provides the solution for our problems. Pride and stubbornness distort the importance of God's authority in our lives.

Self-Will

Associated with pride and stubbornness is self-will. The dangerous aspect of this veil is that it is a very religious thing. In the natural world, self-will is a positive thing. But when it is brought into a church context, it can be devastating.

Self-will always usurps God's will. On the surface, it seems very nice, but just cross self-willed people and watch what happens. Let something challenge anyone's self-will, including our own, and see how nice it really is. Self-will distorts the smiling face of God and veils the fact that God's will has our best interest in mind for the long run. Self-will is only concerned about now.

Religious Ambition

Religious ambition is probably the most deceptive of all the veils. A person can be very religiously ambitious. We see this all the time. Unfortunately, religious ambition usually distorts the will of God.

It works something like this. Most people want their church to grow and be a mighty force for God in their community. And this is admirable. But along comes a religiously ambitious person who generates so much excitement among the people that they forget what their purpose in the community is all about. It is not bigness that God honors. In fact, most of the time huge crowds hinder what God really wants to do.

Some pastors are pushing their churches beyond the scope of divine authority. Some churches are more into politics. Some are more into the social concerns. For other churches, the great interest is education. All of these things are good but not one of them is part of the commission God gave the Church. Simply because a person cloaks something with religious terminology does not make that thing an approved work of God.

Religious ambition easily distorts and veils the approval of God upon a company of people.

Claims of Ownership

Here is where we get into a lot of difficulty. Whatever I claim for myself becomes a veil obscuring God from my view. What I do not absolutely surrender and give up to God comes between God and me. Some Christians believe that if they fast enough and pray about something long enough, God will change His mind about a certain thing. That has never been the case. Not all the fasting and prayer in the world can remove this veil.

Once I put everything on the altar and leave it there, the brightness of God's smiling face will be seen. I think after Abraham relinquished any claim he had on Isaac, he looked at the world in a very different fashion. What you hang on to will weigh you down and hinder you in your pursuit of spiritual perfection.

Fear

The father of fear is unbelief. Fear distorts the smiling aspect of God's face. Do I really believe that God has my best in mind? Or is there a bit of fear in my heart obscuring His good intentions? My circumstances are no indication of whether the smiling favor of God is upon me. Fear causes me to look around at my circumstances instead of up at the smiling face of God.

If the three Hebrew children in the fiery furnace had been more conscious of the fire around them than that God was with them, they might have felt discouraged. But they looked beyond the fire and saw the smiling face of God. They were so conscious of God and His favor on them that the Scriptures tell us that when they came out of the fire, not a hair on their bodies was singed and their clothes did not have the smell of smoke (see Dan. 3:27).

Money

Money is another great veil that obscures God's face from the believer. How easy it is to be entangled in a web of finances. This includes not only having a lot of money but also not having enough money. Solomon wisely said:

> Two things have I required of thee; deny me them not before I die: Remove far from me vanity and lies: give me neither poverty nor riches; feed me with food convenient for me: Lest I be full, and deny thee, and say, Who is the LORD? or lest I be poor, and steal, and take the name of my God in vain (Prov. 30:7-9).

The veil of money has never been about how much money you have but rather about how much money has you. For most of us, it does not take very much money to obscure the smiling face of God. Whatever gets between you and God is all that is needed.

Friendships

Friendship is the most difficult veil and the one that causes us the most grief. Our friendships can get between God and us. I am not thinking just of our friendships with unsaved people. My experience has been that following my conversion to Christ, my unsaved friends left me. What I am mainly thinking of are the friendships we have within the Church. Sometimes those friendships become more important to us than our relationship with God.

The problem here is that there is a great deal of pressure for us to adjust to one another. The common denominator is ourselves. We are called not to adjust ourselves to one another but to adjust ourselves to God. Nothing is more wonderful and encouraging than Christian fellowship, but when that fellowship begins to replace our fellowship with God—and that can easily happen—it becomes a veil of obscurity.

Our Social Position

For many of us, this is the hardest veil to take down. For the most part, we establish our identities by the positions we hold. These positions then determine our influence in the church and in the community. We do not have to hold a major position or a high-paying one. It may even be a position that you volunteer to do. The danger lurks in allowing our position to replace God's approval in our lives. Man's approval can distort God's approval.

Take Down the V

These veils are all aspects of life that ...
nocent but certainly can become something
face of God. Some Christians get this. Some un...
truth of this and are doing something about it. But oth...
be like the Israelites. They will come up to Kadesh-Barnea on...
a week for years and then turn around and go back into the
wilderness. Then they will wonder why there is so much sand
in their shoes.

Simply put, they will not go on beyond Kadesh-Barnea.
They will not advance to the Promised Land. Moving forward
toward a crucified life will take some work and commitment
on our part, and one of the things we need to do is to take
down our veils of obscurity so that the sunshine of God's
smiling face is upon us.

The face of God is always smiling, and not all the veils I
mentioned or even the devil can stop Him from smiling in our
direction. The devil can blow up a storm and put it between
us and the face of God, but God is still smiling. Remember,
God is waiting for you to move up to see His smile. We are the
ones who put up the veils that obscure the view.

Have No Rivals to God

Our God is a jealous lover and suffers no rival. Whatever rival
you construct becomes an obstruction between you and your
God. I do not say that you are not joined to Him and that you
are not justified by grace. I say that this wondrous divine illumination, this ability to perfectly love Him and worthily
praise Him, becomes veiled. It gets choked out and smitten
down, and for a generation now, it has not even been taught.

If you will take the veils down and put them under your
feet, you will discover they hide all that bothers you. All that

ries you will be gone, and there will be nothing but the ean sky above. Christ does not have to die again. No cross will ever need to be erected again. Nothing needs to be added to the atonement. The face of God continues to smile on His people; however, there is a cloud, a veil, hiding that face and that smile.

Don't Be Cheated

Some people say that backsliding is true of sinners but could never be true of Christian people. It may be true of the masses, but it is not true of us. But Christians nowadays have been taught that they can rush to get their little hearts beating and get a fuzzy warm feeling from the hillbilly songs and grand theatrics and all the rest that make up worship in many modern churches.

I don't blame them. But they have been cheated, and the religious leaders have lied to them and wronged them just as in the days of Jesus. Jesus walked among the leaders of His day with His eyes bright and His vision keen and He said to them, "Whatever they say and do may be theologically right, but don't be like them." The leaders responded by saying, "We will kill that man." And they did kill Him. But on the third day, He rose again. Then He sent down the Holy Spirit into this world, and He is yours and mine.

Create No Limits for the Holy Spirit

Do not let anybody tell you how much you can have of the Holy Spirit. Only God can tell you how much you can have of Him. False teachers tell you not to get excited and not to get fanatical, but don't listen to them.

The last generation has been led in evangelical and gospel-church circles. That which is now fundamentalism will become liberalism in a short time. We must have the Holy Spirit back in our churches. We have to have the face of God shining down and the candles of our souls burning bright. We must sense and feel and know the wondrous divine illumination of the One who said, "I am the light of the world" (John 8:12).

Does saying this make me a fanatic? If that is fanaticism, then oh, God, send us more fanaticism. Real fanaticism is when you go against the Scriptures and add things and misinterpret the Word of God. But there is not one line of the Word of God that has been misinterpreted by what I am saying here. It is all based on the doctrine of the faith—the faith of our fathers that is living still.

Stop Wandering

The question is, are you willing to take down the veils of pride and stubbornness, self-will, religious ambition, ownership claims, fear, money, friendships and societal position? Are you willing to tuck them away under your feet?

Perhaps you have been under these veils for a long time. You've tried to pray your way around them, but it does not work that way. You must put these veils under your feet and rise above them. You must put all these things that exist between you and the peace of God away and look into the sunlight. Then relax. There is nothing more you can do. Our God waits, optimistically wanting to help you. He is willing to do it; He is anxious to do it, in fact.

Don't sit back and let yourself become discouraged. You may have been to so many altars and have read so many books that you became confused. Take down the veils between you and God and bask in the sunshine of His everlasting smile. For until God's people put the veils under their feet, nothing will ever happen.

I Take, He Undertakes
A. B. Simpson (1843–1919)

I clasp the hand of Love divine,
I claim the gracious promise mine,
And add to His my countersign,
"I take"—"He undertakes."

I take Thee, blessed Lord,
I give myself to Thee,
And Thou, according to Thy word,
Dost undertake for me.

I take salvation full and free,
Through Him who gave His life for me,
He undertakes my all to be,
"I take"—"He undertakes."

I take Him as my holiness,
My spirit's spotless, heavenly dress,
I take the Lord, my righteousness,
"I take"—"He undertakes."

I take the promised Holy Ghost,
I take the power of Pentecost,
To fill me to the uttermost,
"I take"—"He undertakes."

I take Him for this mortal frame,
I take my healing through His Name,
And all His risen life I claim,
"I take"—"He undertakes."

I simply take Him at His word,
I praise Him that my prayer is heard,
And claim my answer from the Lord,
"I take"—"He undertakes."

11

THE STRANGE
INGENUITY OF THE
CHRISTIAN

I can do all things through Christ which strengtheneth me.
PHILIPPIANS 4:13

The objective before us is to know Christ. We are to learn of Him, to know the power of Christ's resurrection, to be conformed onto His death, to experience in us that which we have in Christ. In order to do that, we must "count all things but loss for the excellency of [this] knowledge."

Allow me to go out on a limb and state something that I have no way of knowing for sure; it's a shrewd guess based on knowing spiritual laws. This is, simply, that once a person begins this journey of living the crucified life, during the first phase of that journey he will experience some of the worst weeks of his life. It is at this point that many will get discouraged and turn back. Those who persevere will find that instead of breaking into the clear bright sunshine, just ahead of them are more discouragements, doubts and deceptions.

Instead of lifting you up, this kind of teaching will cast you down. But let me say this: Those who have been so discouraged—those who have bumped their foreheads on the ceiling or scraped their chins on the sidewalk—and have gone down in some kind of defeat are the very ones who are getting nearer to God. Those who are unaffected—those who can still be worldly and not mind it—have made the least progress. But those who have found things going against them—those who in their longing and yearning for the crucified life, those who wait for Jesus Christ to lead them and instead wonder if He is discouraging them—they probably don't realize that they are very close to the kingdom of God.

"Simply by Grace He May See"

I want to give you another little phrase: "Simply by grace he may see." Or, to put it in modern English, "Let those see who can see by the grace of God." Or, to put it in the language of the Bible, "He that hath ears to hear, let him hear" (Matt 11:15; Mark 4:9; Luke 8:8).

I differ a little from the anonymous author of *The Cloud of Unknowing.* If people could not see, he simply walked out on them. He said, in effect, "I don't want to see janglers and money lovers. I don't want them to even look at my book." He was rather hard-nosed about this point.

I am a little more broad-minded than that. I am going to say that God sifts out those who cannot see in order to lead on by grace those who can see. Remember, even though the number of Chosen People be as the sands of the sea, only a remnant will be saved (see Gen. 22:17; Ezek. 6:8). Although many may wax cold, there is always a remnant.

We read the life of Adoniram Judson and say, "God, I want You to do that to me." We read of D. L. Moody's life and say, "Lord, I want You to do for me what You did to Moody." We want to tell God how to do it, and at the same time we want to reserve a little bit of the glory and have some areas in our life uncrucified. What we really want is a technical crucifixion. We are very happy to listen to another exposition on the sixth chapter of Romans on how we are crucified with Christ, but few people in reality truly want it.

Until we put ourselves in the hands of God and let God do with us as He wills, we will be just what we are—mediocre Christians singing happy songs to keep from being completely blue and trying to keep up the best we can. And while we're doing this, we will not be making any progress toward a crucified life and will not know what it is to be one with Him experientially. Our hearts must be cleansed and our true intent must be to perpetually love Him and worthily praise Him. Then we may be filled with His Spirit and walk in victory.

You do not know what it means to look on God and then go away, letting Him have His way with your life. You are afraid of that. You hope He is all right, you believe He is all right, and you know that the Bible says, "God so loved"; but still you are afraid that if you leave your life in God's hands, something bad will happen.

"See who by grace may see." Let us sit around, get old and wait for the undertaker. Go to conferences year after year and get nothing out of them. Listen to sermons year after year without learning anything. Study the Bible year after year but not make any progress and be just barely able to keep our chins above the water. We are strangely ingenious in fixing our Christian lives so that we get a little glory out of it and get our own way instead of getting God's way.

François Fénelon made an interesting observation: "We are strangely ingenious in perpetually seeking our own interest; and what the world does nakedly and without shame, those who desire to be devoted to God do also, but in a refined manner." This would be humorous if it weren't true. Evidently, the man who could not invent anything *can* invent a way of seeking his own interests.

The Five Ingenious Ways of Christians

There seem to be five ways that we have fallen into this strange ingenuity. The first is by *seeking our own interests while pursuing spiritual interests under the guise of seeking God's interests.* Being self-serving is where the strange ingenuity of Christians begins. Under the guise and pretense of seeking God's interest, we have a sly way of serving our own interests. We have become very clever in this endeavor. But we are only fooling ourselves into thinking that we are "about our Father's business" when we are actually doing our own business.

A pastor may talk about building the church and going around doing kingdom work for the glory of God. He may be quite eloquent about this, but what he is actually doing is shamelessly promoting himself while saying, "I'm doing this for Jesus' sake." When it comes right down to it, it is really his work, his influence, his ambition. That is why he is really doing it.

Musicians can go about a music ministry under the guise of serving the Lord while the same time promoting themselves. There is a fine line between promotion of self and exaltation of Christ. That line sometimes becomes so faint that people do not really know which side of it they are on. While pretending to seek the interest of God, they fall prey to promoting themselves. We want God to have the glory, but at the same time we would like a little commission paid to us for all the work we do. After all, God is "using us for His glory"; and we *do* have to make a living.

A second way is by *talking about the cross and living in the shadow of the cross, but never actually surrendering to it.* I do not find many people talking about the cross these days. But the few that do mention the cross seem only to live in the shadow of that teaching. They never actually fully surrender to the cross as an instrument of death to self. We want to die on the cross, but at the last minute, we always seem to find a way to rescue ourselves.

Nothing is easier to talk about than dying on the cross and surrendering ourselves, but nothing is harder than actually doing it. Talk is cheap, but the walk is what really matters. Some Christians have painted the cross in broad romantic strokes. The fully surrendered life is glamorized and popularized, but it is rarely realized. We can talk ourselves up to the cross, but at the last minute we always seem to find a reason to back down.

A third way is by *begging for the Holy Spirit to fill us while at the same time rejecting Christ's work in us* and *keeping things well in our own hands.* I find that another strange ingenuity among Christians is in the area of the Holy Spirit. It would be difficult to find a Christian not interested in being filled with the Holy Spirit. Of course, a variety of definitions of this doctrine have been floating around for years and clouding the clear teaching of the Word of God. That put aside for the moment, every Christian *does* desire to be filled with the Holy Spirit. I even find some Christians who ask God to fill them with the Holy Spirit. The only problem is that when God begins to move upon them, they reject that move.

They want God to take full control of their lives, but at the same time, they want to keep everything within their own control. The Holy Spirit will never fill a man or a woman who refuses to give up and give over to Him all control of their entire lives. Keep one compartment of your life back from the Holy Spirit, and it grieves Him that He cannot go any further.

Again, there are romantic ideas floating around about the work of the Holy Spirit in the life of the believer. But I want to emphasize that the work of the Holy Spirit can sometimes be harsh and routine. Before a field can be planted, it has to be plowed, and the plowing is harsh and deep. Similarly, there are things in my life that need to be uprooted, and that is exactly what the Holy Spirit wants to do.

We, on the other hand, want to give our lives over to the Holy Spirit, but at the same time, we want to control what the Holy Spirit does in our lives. We want to sit in the control room. We want to issue the commands and the "Thus saith the Lord." I have long concluded that the Holy Spirit works alone in my heart and needs no help from me, other than me simply surrendering absolutely to Him.

A fourth way that we fall into this strange ingenuity is by *talking about the dark night of the soul but rejecting the darkness*. I have read articles and even books dealing with this old theme of "the dark night of the soul." It soon becomes apparent after reading a little bit that most of the authors have no idea what the dark night of the soul really is. And this is where the strange ingenuity of the Christian comes into play. We embrace the dark night of the soul and, at the same time, we reject the darkness.

The dark night of the soul is not something pleasant to go through and does not end with a fellowship supper after church on Sunday night. It is a grueling experience that requires an absolutely strict detachment from everything that you normally rely on so that you are left with only Christ.

The dark night of the soul separates those who are genuinely interested in following Christ from those who just have a curiosity about the "deep things of God." We surely want God to do His work in our lives, but we want the lights left on. We want God to do in our hearts and lives that which will bring Him honoring glory, but we want to know and understand every step that He takes in our lives.

Darkness speaks of not knowing. We want God to *do*, but we want Him to do what He does within the scope of our comprehension. The dark night of the soul, however, is work of the Holy Spirit that exceeds the ability of any man or woman to understand. When we come through the dark night of the soul, we do not know what has really happened to us, but we do know who has made it happen.

A final way is by *using religion to promote our personal interests and advancement*. This is another strange ingenuity of the Christian. It amazes me just how religious people can get. Even the person who has rejected God in Christ and the Church seems to have a strong religious backbone that keeps him steady. But this use of religion for self can also be seen within the Church, in those who have embraced Christ and walk in the light of His Word.

We want to be involved in the work of the Lord, but we want to also be *known* as that faithful servant of the Lord. We want to do God's work, but we want people to know that we are doing God's work. We are ingenious and dream up religious ideas that have no other function than to advance someone's career.

We are perfectly willing to be as religious as possible as long as we can promote ourselves. It may seem strange, maybe even almost humorous, but it is one of the most damning elements operating in the Church today. It is what is robbing this generation of Christians of the spirituality needed to advance the kingdom of God. Perhaps the strangest example of this ingenuity in today's Christianity is seen in the aspect of religious entertainment and personalities, which promote man at the expense of God.

The Cure at the Cross

The only cure for our worldliness is the cross. We cannot put ourselves on the cross. We cannot choose the cross on which we will be crucified. Fénelon speaks of the various kinds of crosses—gold, silver, brass, wood, paper. The one thing they all have in common is that they crucify. How the cross will be used in your life is at the discretion of the Holy Spirit.

If I were to choose my cross and the time of my crucifixion, I would always choose the lesser of two evils. But when the Holy Spirit chooses, He chooses both the time of the crucifixion and the cross upon which He will crucify us. Our responsibility is to yield to His wisdom and allow Him to do the work without any advice from us.

At the Cross I'll Abide
Isaiah Baltzell (1832–1893)

O Jesus, Savior, I long to rest,
Near the cross where Thou hast died;
For there is hope for the aching breast;
At the cross I will abide.

At the cross (At the cross) I'll abide, (I'll abide,)
At the cross (At the cross) I'll abide, (I'll abide,)
At the cross I'll abide,
There His blood is applied
At the cross I am satisfied.

My dying Jesus, my Savior, God,
Who hast borne my guilt and sin,
Now wash me, cleanse me with Thine own blood,
Ever keep me pure and clean.

O Jesus, Savior, now make me Thine,
Never let me stray from Thee;
Oh, wash me, cleanse me, for Thou art mine,
And Thy love is full and free.

The cleansing pow'r of Thy blood apply,
All my guilt and sin remove;
Oh, help me, while at Thy cross I lie,
Fill my soul with perfect love.

12

ALLOWING GOD TO BE HIMSELF

Not that I speak in respect of want: for I have learned,
in whatsoever state I am, therewith to be content.

PHILIPPIANS 4:11

When God said, "Let us make man in our own image," He put an insurmountable gulf between men and every other creature. From God's point of view, man is the highest form of creation. (God also bestowed on man above all other creatures the ultimate honor of His Son, whom He sent in the form of a man.) Something in man responds to something in God, which is a mystical link that no other creature possesses. So in order to know and understand man, we must come to an intimate knowledge of God.

You can put a statue of a person in a park; you can write his name on the walls of famous buildings; you can give the Nobel Peace prize and every kind of prize you can think of to him. But when it has all been said and done, you cannot say anything more of that person than God gave him a certain kind of life, a certain group of habits and a certain environment to be raised in—all are from God. Even the angels, archangels and seraphims cannot say anything more than that about themselves.

Ultimately, though, no matter who we are, we are as poverty stricken as the rest of mankind because we are afraid to use our religious imagination and afraid to believe what the Bible teaches us. The Bible talks about angels, archangels, seraphims, cherubims, watchers, holy ones, principalities and powers. However, we insist on only people; that is all. We are afraid to rise and let our faith-filled imagination enjoy the wonder of the universe.

Man is not like all the other creatures in God's creation. Man fulfills a role that no other creature can fulfill. As long as each living creature stays in its own environment and lives the kind of life God gave it, that creature fulfills that purpose for which it was made.

The creatures on the earth, in the air and in the sea all live in perfect harmony within their own environment. Day by day, they fulfill the purpose for which they were created by simply being themselves in the environment that God put them. Man is the only creation that is out of his original environment.

Roadblocks to Knowing God

An old German theologian once said, "There is nothing in the universe so much like God than the human soul." Everything in the Bible rests upon this truth. God created man with a soul, and in that soul is the capacity to know God and fellowship with God unlike any other creation.

Part of our worship experience is to rise up in a Spirit-filled imagination, see through the eyes of faith and look on God in adoring wonder and amazement. With our feet firmly rooted in the Scriptures, we can rise to that mysterious height of spirituality and become so God conscious that we lose a sense of all other things. Oh, to be lost in the wonder that is God! That is our spiritual heritage. That is the fullness of our redemption in Jesus Christ.

We must accept that as part of our creation and not fear that if we believe it, somebody will charge us with believing that man is all right. Man is not all right. Man is a fallen creature. Man is like an automobile that left the highway at a curve and rolled down among the rocks. Man is not all right. Man is lost.

I often hear preachers talk about a poor, lost, damned soul. No, never call yourself damned. You are lost if you are not converted. You are lost, but you are not damned. That is another thing altogether.

God created man to know Him, and to know Him in a fuller degree than any other creature can know God. No other creature has Christ, and no other creature has the capacity to know God.

The angels have certain capacities. They are holy and obey God. The seraphim sit around the throne and know God, but they do not know God as man knows God. God meant for man to be higher than the angels, and He made him in such a way that, for a little while, he is lower than the angels so that He might raise him higher than the angels. When it is all over and we are known as we are known, we will rise higher in the hierarchy of God than the very angels themselves.

Man lost his way because of his sin. We read about this in Romans 1:21: "Because that, when they knew God, they glorified him not as God, neither were thankful; but became vain in their imaginations and their foolish heart was darkened." Man, by his sin, has lost his knowledge of God. He has the potentiality to know God in a way no other creature can, but he still does not know Him because his conduct is unworthy and his heart is filled with a huge emptiness.

This is the reason we have crises all the time. We have lost our way and flounder in a sea of uncertainty.

Not Seeking the God Who Exists
What is the matter with mankind? We have been created to know God, but because of sin we have become vain in our imaginations. We do not like to have God in our knowledge. We have replaced God with everything but God. We have created a God out of our own imaginations.

This is the state of unregenerate man, but what I want to know is why Christians know Christ and God so little. I understand why the unregenerate man flounders in uncertainty, but why is it that the one creation of God who was created in His image knows very little about his Creator?

I can boil it all down to one sentence: We do not allow God to be Himself. We have lost all sense of knowing God as He is, and consequently we try to make God out to be what He is not. Instead of accepting the fact that we were created in His image, we have deteriorated to the point of believing that God has been created in *our* image.

God is not like us. We, however, are like Him because we have been created in His image. Why then the disparity? Why then this all-but-insurmountable gulf between God and us?

My thoughts on this matter are not the result of my advancement in years. I thought this way when I was converted at 17. At that time, I certainly did not have it developed this far, but over time I went back to the roots of my being. I studied the truths of Christianity. That is the wonderful thing about learning about our God: You can go back to the ancient fountain of our belief and read it over and over again. And then you'll know God for yourself all over again—where Adam started, and back further to where the world began, and back beyond that to where the angels began, and back to that ancient glorious fountain we call the being of God. And in Jesus Christ, we go back there as well.

You cannot know God like you know the multiplication tables or Morse code. You can know almost anything. However, when Paul said, "That I may know him" (Phil. 3:10), he did not mean intellectually but experientially. This means that to know God personally, my spirit must touch His spirit and my heart must touch His heart. Then I will experience the conscious knowledge of God.

It is one thing to hear about this concept but another thing to have lived that concept. It is one thing to hear that there has been a planet suddenly discovered but quite another thing to live on that planet. I can claim that I can know as much about a place by reading about it as most people who will go there. But everybody who goes to a place and comes back is all smiles for having actually been there. If you have actually been there, you know it in a way you cannot know it if you just read about it in a book.

The best unregenerate man can do is know about God. He can study the heavens and see the handiwork of God. The vastness of the universe reveals the unlimited nature of God. A delicate little flower blooming in the spring reveals the tenderness of God. All about us are indications of what God is like. But nothing in nature enables us to enjoy the intimacy of fellowship with God.

We can think of His attributes and rejoice in His grace. But the unregenerate can only do it as an academic exercise. For the unbeliever, God can only be understood through the lens of the microscope. God can only be examined in the laboratory of science. But it is only in a heart quickened by the Holy Spirit that God can really be known.

Settling for Secondhand Knowledge

With all our education, we still do not know God Himself very well. We do not know what fellowship we can have with Him. We leave each other all the time. We get together for fellowship and religious activities and all the religious prompts and lean one on the other, and then we walk away. Jesus said that He had His work to do; He had His healings, opening and unstopping ears, and answering questions. But He also had a personal knowledge of God that was intimate, and He was always able to lean on God.

Modern Christians are so busy doing this and doing that, going here and going there, that they know God only by hearsay. We hear of this and that, but we never hear it said for ourselves. We too easily settle for substitutes rather than the real thing. Under these circumstances, the most we can expect to hear is the indistinguishable echo of God's voice.

Wanting Things Instead of God

Another reason why Christians know Christ and God so little is that we want things instead of God. We are more interested in the gift than the giver. God wants to give us Himself. God wants to impart Himself *with* His gift. Separated from God, the gift is dangerous.

Living with Sins

The thing that stands the most in our way to this intimacy with God is, simply put, sin. The short route to intimacy with God is forgiveness of sins. The importance of this one thing in the life of the believer is vastly underestimated. Sin is responsible for our problems. Sin is the reason we were given such Scriptures as 1 John 1:9: "If we confess our sins, he is faithful and just to forgive us our sins, and to cleanse us from all unrighteousness."

The question that we should be asking is, why does God forgive sin? He forgives sin because sin is the roadblock that stands between us and Him. If we are ever going to know God, the roadblock has to be removed. So God can forgive sin. Why does God pour out His Spirit on us? In order that the Spirit can come and show us the things of God. Why does God answer prayer? In order that in answering prayer He might unveil His own face to us.

Relying on the Bible as an End in Itself

Why has God given us the Scriptures? It is by reading the Scriptures that we might know God. But the Scriptures are not an end in themselves. We hear them talked about as though they were an end in themselves. No man can believe more in the verbal inspiration of the Scriptures as originally given than I do. But verbal inspiration or any other theory of inspiration that makes the Bible an end in itself is a dangerous thing. The purpose of the Bible is not to replace God; the purpose of the Bible is to lead us to God.

The Bible is *never* an end in itself. I pray that God will raise up somebody that is able to make the Orthodox Church, the Bible people, the fundamentalists, the evangelicals, see and understand this. Remember that God Himself said that He was "a jealous God" (Exod. 20:5). We do not want anything or anybody to even remotely take His place.

Pathways to Knowing God

The only Christians you want to listen to are the ones who give you more of a hunger for God. You cannot know all that God has, but you can know all that God has revealed in Christ to your soul, which is infinitely more than you now know. When the Church of Christ returns to teaching this—when it gets serious, stops fooling around and begins to preach God Himself and all of the gifts of God—God will come along with Himself. All the blessings of God will come along with God. We want the fullness of the Spirit to fill us, we want godly living, we want a love divine, we want all of that, but if we keep those things apart from God Himself, we have only found a rose with a thorn.

If you find God, then you find all these things in God. You now say, "I've accepted Christ," and that is very wonderful and good. Paul had been converted and was one of the world's great Christians, but he still wrote: "That I may know him, and the power of his resurrection, and the fellowship of his sufferings, and be made conformable unto his death" (Phil. 3:10).

Everybody wants to know what the deeper life is, what living the crucified life is all about. I almost avoid speaking about this topic anymore, because people talk about the crucified life and the deeper life, but nobody seems to want God. As I come further into the knowledge of the triune God, my heart moves further out into God and God moves further into me. To know God is to experience a deeper life in God. Anything that keeps me from knowing God is my enemy. And any gift that comes between Him and me is an enemy.

I do not believe in keys, per se, but if there ever were a key to unlock the mystery of living the crucified life, it is simply this: Allow God to be Himself. This may seem like a simple thing. But if it were, Christians would not need encouragement to press on to spiritual perfection.

Christians are infamous for trying to put God in a box. The God who fits in a box is not the God and Father of our Lord Jesus Christ. The God who fits in the box is the God who can be controlled by man and who is at the beck and call of man. But this is not the God of the Bible. The God of the Bible is an awesome and mighty force in this universe—the God who created the heavens and the earth and everything that is—and He cannot be put in a little box created by mere man.

When we insist on allowing God to be Himself, there comes within our inner being an explosion of reality regarding the person of Jesus Christ. Our understanding of Him goes beyond academics and into that marvelous world of personal intimacy.

Perhaps the ultimate truth here is that when we allow God to be Himself, we then—and only then—discover who and what we are as men and women. We are then well on our way to living crucified lives.

My Lord, How Full of Sweet Content
Madame Guyon (1647–1717)

My Lord, how full of sweet content;
I pass my years of banishment!
Where'er I dwell, I dwell with Thee,
In heaven, in earth, or on the sea.

To me remains nor place nor time;
My country is in every clime;
I can be calm and free from care
On any shore, since God is there.

While place we seek, or place we shun
The soul finds happiness in none;
But with a God to guide our way,
'Tis equal joy, to go or stay.

Could I be cast where Thou are not,
That were indeed a dreadful lot:
But regions none remote I call,
Secure of finding God in all.

PART IV

THE BLESSINGS
OF THE
CRUCIFIED LIFE

13

THE BEAUTY OF CONTRADICTIONS

I am crucified with Christ: nevertheless I live; yet not I, but Christ liveth in me: and the life which I now live in the flesh I live by the faith of the Son of God, who loved me, and gave himself for me.

GALATIANS 2:20

A casual reading of the Scriptures could bring one to the conclusion that there are contradictions in the Bible. The enemies of the Bible have worked overtime to bring all of these apparent contradictions to light. Perhaps of all the "contradictions" in the Bible, no other author of the New Testament has been accused of contradicting himself more often than the apostle Paul.

Take for example what the apostle Paul says in 2 Corinthians 12:10: "Therefore I take pleasure in infirmities, in reproaches, in necessities, in persecutions, in distresses for Christ's sake: for when I am weak, then am I strong." What could be more contradictory? Paul says that when he is weak, then he is strong. This is obviously a great contradiction. How can you be strong when you are weak? And how can you put the word "pleasure" in the same sentence as "infirmities," "reproaches," "necessities," "persecutions" and "distresses"? No man in his right mind would associate these things with each other.

That is exactly the point: Paul is not in his "right mind." He is actually operating and ministering through the mind of Christ. What makes sense in the human mind does not make sense in the spiritual mind. And what makes sense in the spiritual mind seems to be contradictory to the natural man's mind or even the mind of the carnal man.

Two Contradictory Schools of Thought

Contradictory elements can be found even among Christians today. Within the framework of Christendom are two contradictory schools of thought. I am not referring to Calvinism and Arminianism, nor am I thinking of liberalism and fundamentalism. I'm referring to the reason we think Jesus came into the world.

Jesus Came to Help Us

The one school of thought holds that the Lord Jesus Christ came into this world in order to help us. That is, to take us out of the conflicts and the twisted situations we get into during our lives. The thinking is that we are all right except for a few twists and turns here and there, which surely the Lord can straighten out. Man is basically good except for a few little mistakes now and then.

This thinking also holds that the purpose of Christianity is to make us better people. By being Christians, we can be more popular and successful out in the world. No matter what our business is, Christianity and the teachings of Jesus could make us successful in it. For example, if you are a nightclub singer in the cesspools of the world, God will help you be the best nightclub singer you could possibly be. If you are running a crooked business, why, the Lord will help you to be successful and popular at that as well.

Believing this line of thought takes all of the supposedly good things in Scripture and claims them for ourselves. God simply wants to make us a good man (or woman). Feelings of low self-esteem can be quickly eradicated by believing that in Jesus, we can be the best we can possibly be. No matter what our problem is, Christ can make it go away. Christianity, according to this school of thought, is a sort of deluxe edition of life and helps improve the all-important self-esteem issues that we might have. It helps us to feel better about ourselves, which is viewed as the ultimate goal of all religion.

This "feel-better" Christianity has fostered an entire new industry of religious self-help. All you need to have a bestseller these days is the claim that what you say will help people feel better about themselves. Christianity is simply a huge following of people who believe that the teachings of Jesus in the Scriptures can help their self-images, bolster their egos and make them happy and cheerful. Visit any bookstore and you will see shelves of books written to encourage this type of thinking about Christianity.

To people who believe Jesus came only to help them—and this is what causes my heart to ache—Jesus died on the cross and suffered such intense pain and agony just so average Christians could feel better about themselves. Entire ministries today are devoted to this sort of thing, which has morphed into Christian "entertainmentism."

Instead of preaching sermons that "stir up your pure minds by way of remembrance" (2 Pet. 3:1), we now must entertain the congregation with the latest forms of entertainment available. Today's evangelical church is filled with entertainment toys of all sorts: projectors, bands, lights, noise—everything to capture the attention of poor, immature, underdeveloped Christians. If it rattles, if it is frivolous, if it makes a person laugh, it is accepted in the Church today with open arms.

If some local church decides to put away all of these entertainment toys and focus on Bible preaching and teaching, the crowds are sure to find another church, one that will tickle their fancy. Discipleship has given way to building self-esteem.

It is not so much what you know as it is how you look and feel that is important. This form of Christianity is not rooted in biblical truth but in cultural relativity, the aggrandizement of materialism. But woe be to the church that is not relevant to the surrounding culture.

To be fair, the temptation is too great for some pastors, and they succumb to the whims of the flesh. As long as the entertainment is "clean," it must be all right. But in my mind, to substitute intense worship of God for carnal entertainment is to misunderstand completely what it means to be a Christian.

It goes without saying that this type of thinking about Christianity satisfies the flesh. As long as the flesh is respectable, it is accepted in the Church these days. If it draws a crowd, it must be okay. If the people want it, why not give it to them? After all, so the reasoning goes, whatever it takes to get them in is all right as long as we can share Jesus with them. But I wonder what Jesus they are sharing with this crowd who wants their flesh satisfied.

I must point out here that "self" has done many good things in this world. It has built hospitals, orphanages, fed the hungry and clothed the poor. Self has been busy doing many good works. But the problem with these good works is that self requires the glory for all of these things. Now, if that self is highly religious, it is willing to give God 99 percent of the glory, but it wants to retain at least 1 percent of the glory so that people know what a faithful servant of the Lord the self is. This goes against scriptural teaching that God desires all of the glory. He will not share any percentage of His glory with any man.

Jesus Came to Put an End to Self

The other school of thought among Christians is that Jesus Christ came to bring an end to self. Not educate it or polish it, but put an end to it. Not cultivate it, give it a love for Bach, Plato and da Vinci, but to bring an end to self. This position pronounces a death sentence on everything related to self, or the ego. The apostle Paul set the standard when he said, "Not I, but Christ" (Gal. 2:20). The "I" must be eliminated in its entirety for Christ to hold His rightful position in our lives.

I must counsel that any church majoring in this ministry will pay a heavy price. The crowds will not flock to such a ministry, because they are seeking something to satisfy the flesh. They want something frivolous to entertain them, fluff them up and make them feel good about themselves.

But I do not think this is necessarily a negative. Those who do come to such churches possess an insatiable appetite for God and desire above everything else to see Christ glorified in their lives. The glory of God always comes at the sacrifice of self. I would rather have a congregation of 25 who seek to honor God 100 percent and give Him all of the glory than to have a congregation of 2,500 burdened with the curse of "entertainmentism" where God will have to fight for a percentage of the glory. To have God lurking in the shadows of the church is to not have God in that church.

Too many people underestimate the power self has as a distraction and a deception and, ultimately, its power to compromise solid biblical Christianity. The whole burden of New Testament theology is that the old self-values are false, that wisdom of the self is questionable, and that the self's goodness does not exist at all. The old self must go, regardless of the cost. In the old self-life, there is nothing redeemable. No matter how much the old self is cleaned up, it still contains an irredeemable core of corruption.

The new man is in Christ, and from now on we must reckon ourselves to be dead to sin but alive to God in Jesus Christ. The question that presents itself is, how do we deal with the old self?

If it is all that the Scriptures claim it to be, what is to be done with it?

This is where we come to another apparent contradiction in the Scriptures. Galatians 2:20, the key verse for the crucified life, is Paul's testimony, a beautiful type of personal theology thrown into an epistle that is not so beautiful. (The Galatians were known for their backsliding.) In Galatians 2, the apostle placed a little diamond that, in my mind, is at the center of the entire epistle: "I am crucified with Christ: nevertheless I live; yet not I, but Christ liveth in me: and the life which I now live in the flesh I live by the faith of the Son of God, who loved me, and gave himself for me."

Notice that this little verse has a number of contradictions in it. Paul starts the verse, with "I am crucified." On the surface, this looks like a contradiction. We know that no one who has been crucified will live to tell about it. So either Paul had not been crucified and can talk about it, or he had been crucified, in which case he could not talk about it.

No one has ever said, "Doctor, call the undertaker because I have died." If he had not died and was in his right mind, he would not say he had died. And if he had died, he would not be able to tell the doctor anything. Yet here is the apostle Paul saying that he has been crucified, and that in itself is a contradiction.

"Nevertheless I live." I could grant that by some wonder a man could say, "I have been crucified," as though he were speaking from the next world back to this one. But then Paul contradicts himself by saying, "Nevertheless I live." If he had been crucified, how then could he live?

Paul goes on to contradict that and say, "Not I." Then, going on further, he says, "The life which I now live in the flesh (I who have been crucified yet am alive and yet am not alive). And yet not I, but Christ now lives in me. I live in the flesh by the faith of the Son of God who loved me and gave Himself up for me." Talk about contradictions!

I deliberately emphasized the contradictions in this verse not because I believe there are any basic contradictions, but because this verse cannot be passed over when read, as is so often done with the Lord's Prayer or the Twenty-third Psalm. Either the verse means something or it does not. If it means something, I want to know what it means. If it does not mean anything, I ought to find that out and ignore it from here on. I do believe it means something. And not only do I believe it means something, but I also believe that it can be made practical, workable and livable in this present world in the lives of each one of us.

The old "I" must be absolutely crucified. That is what Paul is talking about in Galatians 2:20. Nobody can die partially. Either a person is dead or he is alive. This is much like drinking a glass of water with poison in it. That glass does not have to be filled 100 percent with poison to kill you. Even if only 1 percent of the liquid in the glass is poison, it will do the trick. In fact, it is my opinion that if only 1 percent of the liquid is poison, the glass is the more dangerous because the poison is less obvious. A glass with 100 percent poison will kill you outright. A glass with 1 percent poison will kill you for sure, but your death will be slower and drawn out and more painful.

In our Christian experience, if there is still some small shred of the old "I," the danger is great. That little bit will destroy just as surely as if the entire self were poison.

This is what Paul is talking about. The old self must go in its entirety and the new must come in its entirety. The "I" of the old self is crucified. We are dead, yet we are alive as we have never been alive before. It is not our life but the life of our blessed Redeemer that permeates every essence of our being.

Through this crucifixion of self, the life of Christ *can* be made practical, workable and livable in this present world in the lives of Christians.

"Yet not I, but Christ lives in me" is the most important phrase in Galatians 2:20. It is Christ in me that makes all the difference in the world. And until the old "I" is done away with, the life of Christ cannot come. However, many Christians hang on to the old "I" in desperation. So fearful are they that they might lose something, they forget what Jesus taught: "For whosoever will save his life shall lose it: and whosoever will lose his life for my sake shall find it" (Matt. 16:25). Until we are willing to lose, we will never find what God has for us.

What a great Christianity we evangelicals have these days. The liberals criticize us, and I for one do not blame them. They have a right; they do not have anything better to do. What a bunch of unworthy people we evangelicals have become, daring to stand up on our feet and preach to an intelligent audience that the essence, the final purpose and the cause of Christ is to save us from hell. How stupid can we get and still claim to be followers of Christ?

The purpose of God is not to save us from hell; the purpose of God is to save us to make us like Christ and to make us like God. God will never be done with us until the day we see His face, when His name will be on our foreheads; and we shall be like Him because we shall see Him as He is.

What a cheap, across-the-counter commercial kind of Christianity that says, "I was in debt, and Jesus came and paid my debt." Sure, He did, but why emphasize that? "I was on my way to hell and Jesus stopped me and saved me." Sure, He did, but that is not the thing to emphasize. What we need to emphasize is that God has saved us to make us like His Son. His purpose is to catch us on our wild race to hell, turn us around because He knows us, bring judgment on the old self and then create a new self within us, which is Jesus Christ.

The Beauty of the Lord

The most beautiful verse in the Bible is found in Psalm 90:7: "Let the beauty of the LORD our God be upon us." How wonderful is the beauty of the Lord our God? The sharp contrast to the beauty of the Lord our God is the ugliness of I, myself. The anonymous writer of the *Theologia Germanica* said, "Nothing burns in hell but self-will." That would be the "my," "me," "I" and "mine" that are the fuel of hell.

In the great divine exchange, God offers to trade our old selves, which have brought us so many problems, for new selves, which are Christ. The apostle Paul says, "And the life which I now live in the flesh I live by the faith of the son of God, who loved me, and gave himself for me."

To arrive at this point is well worth the journey. The pain associated with the sacrifice of the old self is nothing compared to the joy of experiencing that afflatus from on high coming down and penetrating every aspect of our life. In the natural world, the crucified life may seem full of contradictions, because the old nature, the self-life, is completely out of step with God and contrary to His nature. But when we crucify the self, God will give us His beauty, His joy, His Son.

Not I, But Christ
Frances E. Bolton (d. 1926)

Not I, but Christ, be honored, loved, exalted,
Not I, but Christ, be seen be known, be heard;
Not I, but Christ, in every look and action,
Not I, but Christ, in every thought and word.

Oh, to be saved from myself, dear Lord!
Oh, to be lost in Thee!
Oh, that it might be no more I,
But Christ that lives in me!

Not I, but Christ, to gently soothe in sorrow,
Not I, but Christ, to wipe the falling tear;
Not I, but Christ, to lift the weary burden,
Not I, but Christ, to hush away all fear.

Christ, only Christ! no idle words e'er falling,
Christ, only Christ; no needless bustling sound;
Christ, only Christ; no self important bearing,
Christ, only Christ; no trace of "I" be found.

Not I, but Christ, my every need supplying,
Not I, but Christ, my strength and health to be;
Not I, but Christ, for body, soul, and spirit,
Christ, only Christ, here and eternally.

Christ, only Christ ere long will fill my vision;
Glory excelling soon, full soon I'll see
Christ, only Christ my every wish fulfilling
Christ, only Christ my all and all to be.

14

The Refreshment
of a Revival

Abide in me, and I in you. As the branch cannot bear fruit of itself,
except it abide in the vine; no more can ye, except ye abide in me.
John 15:4

Perhaps the greatest result of living the crucified life is that periodically it brings us to places of great spiritual victory. Throughout history, these periods have been referred to as revivals. Nothing is more needed right now in the contemporary Church than a revival.

A revival can occur on one of three levels. It can occur on a personal level, when an individual is revived. It can occur on a church level, when the whole church comes under a new spiritual impetus. It can occur on a community level, when a church overflows and the spiritual impetus in the church extends into the community.

A solitary person can enter into revival and have a revitalization of his spiritual life; a surge of power and an infilling of grace that causes him to enter into an experience so wonderful that words cannot describe it. Yet it would not affect the church that he happens to be attending. Within pretty cold churches, there have been greatly revived individuals, yet those churches did not experience revival because the churches opposed, neglected or considered these revived people fanatics or extremists and basically froze them out.

An individual church may experience an awakening, and such a revival impacts all of the individuals in the congregation and might even increase the number of individuals attending the church. People are lifted up and refreshed, and out of the frozen streams the ice breaks and the water begins to flow. Yet it often fails to extend beyond the local church. Many local churches have awakenings and refreshings, but these revivals do not get beyond the church walls into the community.

Then there is such a thing as a community revival where the Word does get into the community, going from one church to another, from one neighborhood to another, until the whole city is revived.

A community revival can start with an individual, extend to the church and extend out to include the community, but it can never occur in the reverse order. It can never begin in the community, unless there has been a church that has been revived, and no churches have ever been revived until individuals in the church have been revived.

Personal Revival

What do I mean by a "personal" revival? The best way I can describe it is that it is like a sick man returning to abundant health. Suppose a man has a blood count that is so low he is hardly able to get out of bed and can only stay up an hour at a time. Then, suddenly, he gets to a place where he is able to do a hard day's work, play on a baseball team and do anything else he wants because he has been restored to abundant health. Or imagine a weak battery that will barely turn a car engine over. Once that battery is recharged, it is filled with power and a spark will fly out from it and start the engine. That is what it means to be revived as a Christian. It is a new, refreshing rush of power from God.

This not only can happen to the individual but also to a church. But it must first happen to individuals in that church. I want to make this very clear, because it is important that we think right about this. There is no abstract idea here. We like to pray, "Oh, Lord, fall on Thy Church." Somehow, we imagine an abstract church somewhere and the Holy Spirit comes down and fills the church without the individuals inside being affected. But the Holy Spirit can only fall on individuals. There is no such thing as a church being blessed without having the members of the church touched. We pray, "Lord, bless Thy abstract Church," and we imagine a church detached from individuals, some sort of ideal church for which Christ died. But God cannot pour His Spirit out on His church unless He first pours it on the individuals within the church. The Holy Spirit "sat upon each of them," and so He will sit upon each of us (Acts 2:3).

Every local church is only as good as the individual members are, not one bit better. If God had some IQ test whereby He could test our faith or He had some way of taking our spiritual pulse, then we might add up all our membership and get the average, and the Church would be whatever the average is. Always remember, though, that the average does not make up the Church, for the Church is composed of individuals.

The lone soul can be revived. I am glad to be able to tell you that. God can send waves of glory, a new quickening to the lone individual. As a solitary individual, whether anyone else in your church receives revival or not, you do not have to wait around and say, "I'd like to see our church blessed," and then hope that when it is blessed you will also be blessed. The church can never be blessed until you or other individuals in your church are blessed. Whether the church gets any further on out or backslides and turns liberal, you can be blessed as an individual, and not all the rest of us put together can prevent that. You alone can be blessed whether or not your pastor personally knows about it.

When I was about 18 years of age, God came on me in a wonderful way and did wonderful things for me, but my church did not approve of it. In fact, they as good as told me that I was a bit extreme and that the church would be better without my company. I was not thrown out; I was just invited not to belong, and I left and went to a Christian and Missionary Alliance church. Whether the church believes or not, you *can* have all that God has for you as an individual. Whether your wife or your husband or father or mother or friend will agree or not does not make a bit of difference. God always is ready to help the lone individual.

The history of the Old Testament is filled with stories of lone individuals—men and women—meeting God. The story of revivals throughout the ages has been the story of lone men meeting God, of going out and finding God all alone. Sometimes they went down to the church basement, sometimes to caves, sometimes out under trees, sometimes by haystacks, but they went alone to meet God, and then the revival went out from there. I say that you, personally, can be blessed and yet not have a revival in your church. If you are attending a church that is suffering a spiritual malaise, a low level of or even a dead spirituality, never lower yourself to match that level. Instead, say to yourself, *By the grace of God, I'm going to be what I should be regardless.*

How to Have a Personal Revival

The big question then is, how can we experience a personal revival? In order to see a fresh outpouring of the Holy Spirit in our lives, there are four things that must be set in order. The work of the Holy Spirit is not capricious; rather, there are some well-defined spiritual rules that govern His work in our lives.

Set Your Face Like Flint

First, if you are going to have a personal revival, you must "set [your] face like a flint" (Isa. 50:7). A plow that is going to be used on sod must have a sharp point. Likewise, if you want a personal revival, you have to have a hard-nose because of all of the schemes and tricks of the world. You must set your face like flint and say, "I go by the grace of God. I want all that the New Testament has for me."

Set Your Heart on Jesus

Second, you must set your heart on Jesus Christ. Wherever He takes you, go with Him. Whatever He takes you away from, listen to Him and follow what He says. Whomever you must ignore, move away from. If you want to be all that God wants you to be, set your face like flint and go straight to Jesus.

I will always thank God that the Bible includes the passage where the blind man said, "Jesus, thou Son of David, have mercy on me" (Mark 10:47). His disciples went out and said to the man, "Be quiet. This is not done in church. Just keep still." Instead of their words discouraging him, it fired him to cry out more, until Jesus turned around and said, "What do you want?"

"I want to be healed."

And Jesus said, "Okay, here's your healing." The man received his eyesight because he paid no attention to the "timekeepers and referees" who served only to keep people away from Jesus.

I recently looked again at John Bunyan's book *Pilgrim's Progress* and read a page or two, more or less for the style than anything else. But you cannot read Bunyan very long just for the style, because the story of Christian and how he got into trouble on his journey is so fascinating.

Early on, Christian says, "I find by this book [the Bible] that I am in great distress. I must leave my hometown of Destruction and journey to a heavenly home." So he plans to start out for that heavenly home. He is in terrible stress before he begins, and he finally breaks down before his children and says, "Oh, my dear wife and children, I've gotten into an awful condition. Just awful."

His family basically replies, "We know what's wrong with you. You're just tired." So they put him to bed, and the next morning he got up and they said to him, "How are you feeling, Father?"

"I didn't sleep a wink. I couldn't forget that we're living in the city of Destruction."

Bunyan says that when Christian's family found that they could not quiet and console him, when they could not pat him on the back and say, "Go back to sleep and sleep it off," they started being harsh toward him and derided him. Then, when he would not give up because of their scorn, they ignored him.

I thought as I read it, *First they soothe you, then they pat you on your back and hope you'll quiet down. After that, they use harsh words, accusing you of thinking you are better than other people. And when that doesn't work, they deride you and start making fun of you. And when that doesn't work, they ignore you.*

That is exactly how it happens when you set your heart on Jesus and seek personal revival. If you decide to seek a deeper relationship with God and meet Him on your own and have a refreshing from God to get rid of the old barnacles and the weights and hindrances and get back a new spirit within you, you will find that some people will say, "Well, you're just excited. You've just allowed that man Tozer to stir you up." John Bunyan said that when Christian was treated like that, he went to be by himself and pray.

Set Yourself Up for Examination

The third thing you must do in order to experience personal revival is expose your life to God's examination. The trouble is that we keep ourselves and cover our hearts. Scripture says, "He that covereth his sins shall not prosper: but whoso confesseth and forsaketh them shall have mercy" (Prov. 28:13). Out of habit, we cover ourselves and try to hide our sins. If you want revival, you must allow the Scriptures to be the Scriptures in your life.

Expose your whole life to Jesus Christ. Expose yourself in prayer. Expose yourself in Scriptures. Expose your heart in obedience. Expose it by confession and by restitution. "Restitution" is a forgotten word today that nobody uses anymore. But it *is* in the Bible. "Restitution" means to get straightened out with people. When you make restitution, you will be amazed at how wonderful you will feel.

Set for Yourself Holy Affirmations

The fourth thing you must do for personal revival is to make some holy affirmations. Several affirmations that I have had to make before God have significantly changed my walk as a Christian. Let me share them with you, and then you take it from there.

Declare before God never to own anything. I do not mean for you to get rid of anything that you can use. I mean you should get rid of that bunch of trash you have in your life. Too many Christians are a bunch of pack rats, gathering everything, going out and bringing everything they can. If you were to find a magpie nest, you would find a variety of things: a mirror, a coat hanger, a piece of glass, maybe a dime. The magpie cannot use those things; the bird just likes them, so it collects them. Similarly, because of a coveting spirit, many Christians collect all around them things that they really cannot use.

Keep in mind that if you feel you own something, it is actually dragging you down. Cut loose from the ownership of that item, and then God will let you have it. Cut loose from inside yourself, and God will let you have the thing on the outside of yourself. This has to do with your automobiles, property, clothes and everything you have collected throughout your life. Take everything and say that God has it. Do not imagine for a minute that if you give God 10 percent, you are okay and you can keep the remaining 90 percent. God must have 100 percent. Once you give it all to Him, then He will make sure you have enough to look after yourself and your family.

If there is anything you own that God cannot have, you never will have a revival. If there is anything that you own that God cannot have, you cannot have God. God has a right to command whatever He wants the moment He wants it. The moment God knows that He can have whatever you have anytime He wants it, then the Lord will probably let you keep it, and it will be a blessing for you instead of a curse. It will help lift you up instead of being an anchor to weigh you down.

Another affirmation that has been important to me is to never defend myself. This is a tough one, particularly for Americans. Through the years, I have taken a great many people to the twenty-third chapter of Exodus to teach them how to trust God and not worry about enemies. If you try to fight people, you will only get bloody and bruised, and you'll feel miserable. You will stay an immature Christian and never have a revival. But if you let God do your fighting for you, you will come out all right.

Another affirmation that has been important to me is to never defame a fellow Christian. By this, I mean never believe evil about him or speak an evil report about him. Remember your past and your own tendency to give in to temptation. I think sometimes the Spirit of God shuts Himself up tight and cannot come on us because we have defamed a brother or sister Christian. Such an evil report becomes a weapon in the devil's hand.

As a pastor and a member of an executive committee, I am forced under God that if I hear charges against a man's life, I am obligated to protect the Church of God from that man. But this does not mean that I will defame that man or any other man by believing gossip or by spreading it.

Another important affirmation is never to receive or accept any glory. Oh, how we love glory. We just want to take a little of it for ourselves. We sing songs attributing glory to God and giving Him all the glory, but sometimes we do not really mean it. We want God to get *most* of the glory, but we would like to reserve just a little bit for ourselves. After all, we believe we have earned it.

Why You Should Seek a Personal Revival

Do not wait for tragedy to drive you to God. Some Christians start to get cold in their hearts and then some tragedy strikes, either to themselves or to their families, and out of that grief they say, "Forgive me, God." They want to start over. But must it always be like that? Must we always wait around for God to chastise us? Must we always come to God with bleeding backs? Determine before God that you will not wait for tragedy to drive you to Him. Take your cross voluntarily.

Many years ago when I was a very young preacher, I preached in a town called Despard, West Virginia. It was commonly called Tinplate because a great tinplate factory was there, but it was also a coal-mining area. I and some others went into that area and had some gospel meetings. The meetings were not exactly what some people thought they should be, and some began to feel burdened by the fact that no revival was taking place. At the meeting one night was a tall, handsome, blond coal miner. He said to his wife, "You know, our people need God. They need God, and this thing isn't going well. Honey, if it's all right with you, I'm going to take tomorrow off and wait on God and pray and fast all day long. I want to wait on God for revival for this town."

Instead of going to work the next day, he got down on his knees and waited on God with an open Bible all day long. The next day he went back to his work on the tipple. (The tipple is where the cars carrying coal are emptied out.) He was working on that tipple and suddenly something went wrong. The car jumped the track, crashed and broke apart. The cars at this mine were old-fashioned wooden ones, and this one broke into splinters sharp as daggers, and one ripped through this man's thigh. It pierced an artery, and this 47-year-old man bled to death on the dirt floor.

Remember, the day before he had spent with God. That struck me as a message from heaven above, and I thought ever since, *Dear God, how wonderful it would be to spend my last day with Thee alone in prayer.*

Now, the coal miner could not take every day off to pray, for he had to work and support his family. But I think it was a wonderful thing that he was so near to God the day before he died. He had unburdened himself to God the night before. You cannot spend all day with God and not be ready to go to heaven the next day.

Do not ask me why God took the dear man away. I will never know that. God never has let me in on all His secret plans. I only know that in the course of things, the man could have died anywhere any day. But the Spirit of God urged him to spend a day in prayer for his own soul and for his church. Suppose he had been too cold to listen or had been too far away to hear? Suppose he had been like someone running on automatic, not listening for God's call? He would have died on the tipple the next day all right, but oh, what a difference.

Maybe God is calling you to do something extraordinary, something that does not appear on your calendar or agenda, something to revive your own soul. Maybe God is calling you to do something radical and extreme for your soul. I hope and pray that the world and the pleasures of it are not so great that you are unable to hear Him. The biggest thing in the world is not whether you live to be 100 years old; the biggest thing in the world is whether you can hear God speaking to you now. That is what counts.

Is God saying anything to you? You can have a revival whether anybody else ever gets one or not. There is no reason why you personally cannot set your face like flint and determine to go wherever Jesus takes you. When you find Him, you will find the floodgates of mercy. You will find fresh oil. You will find a wonderful new revival life for yourself.

Old-Time Power
Paul Rader (1878–1938)

We are gathered for Thy blessing,
We will wait upon our God;
We will trust in Him Who loved us,
And Who bought us with His blood.

Spirit, now melt and move
All of our hearts with love,
Breathe on us from above
With old time power.

We will glory in Thy power,
We will sing of wondrous grace;
In our midst, as Thou has promised,
Come, O come, and take Thy place.

Bring us low in prayer before Thee,
And with faith our souls inspire,
Till we claim, by faith, the promise
Of the Holy Ghost and fire.

15

The Everlasting Rewards of Living the Crucified Life

Behold, how good and how pleasant it is for brethren
to dwell together in unity!

PSALM 133:1

The worth of any journey can always be measured by the difficulties encountered along the way. The more difficult the journey, the more satisfying the destination. I have been thinking of the crucified life as a journey. It has a beginning, of course, but the end is never this side of glory. I am reminded of this thought in a hymn called "The King's Business":

> I am a stranger here within a foreign land;
> My home is far away upon a golden strand;
> Ambassador to be of realms beyond the sea,
> I'm here on business for my King.

Not many Christians consider themselves strangers "within a foreign land." But that is exactly what we are if we are Christians. If we have begun the journey and are living the crucified life, this world certainly is not our home. That is why we should never get too comfortable in this life.

Some people have been misinformed about the Christian life and living the crucified life. For some reason, they think that it is an easy path. They believe that God will take away all of their problems and difficulties and that they will be able to live their lives without any kind of distraction or disturbance. As everybody who has traveled this journey knows, such is not the case. If your journey is not cluttered with difficulties and hardships and burdens, you just might be on the wrong path.

It is impossible to read the Bible and not see that every man and woman of God faced some extreme difficulties and troubles. Church history is also filled with stories of the struggles that believers have had, even beyond what the martyrs of the Church faced. If the Christian life is as easy as some people believe, then why all this history of struggle and difficulty and martyrdom?

Types of Difficulties

Difficulties can fall into several categories. First, difficulties can be a distraction. By "distraction," I mean that they can knock us off our main course. Back on the farm in Pennsylvania, we plowed using a horse. In order for that horse not to be distracted, we had to put blinders on it. It was that easy for a horse to get distracted.

The difficulties that come our way can distract us from our true purpose before God. We can become so immersed in our difficulties that we see nothing else. We can forget the direction we are going. If you study the history of Israel, you will find that their whole journey was filled with distraction after distraction. They would get going in one direction and then something would happen to distract them and pull them either to the left or to the right.

Of course, the difficulties that come our way can make us feel discouraged. Many people have a hard time believing that a Christian could ever get discouraged. When a Christian has difficulties that bring him to a point of discouragement, he is tempted to believe that he hasn't really been born again. The truth of the matter is that the various difficulties that he faces has the potential of shrouding his good sense and clouding him with a good dose of discouragement.

It is quite sad to read or hear of a person who has started out well but somehow got distracted, and that this distraction caused him to stop dead in his tracks. The apostle Paul dealt with this among the Galatian Christians:

> Are ye so foolish? having begun in the Spirit, are ye now made perfect by the flesh? (Gal. 3:3).

The Galatians had started out well, but something along the way had distracted them from their original purpose and brought them to a state of discouragement. They began to feel as though they had to fight their own battles. That is where we also get into trouble. Difficulties are a common aspect of life. But we should be encouraged by what Paul wrote to the Corinthians:

> There hath no temptation taken you but such as is common to man: but God is faithful, who will not suffer you to be tempted above that ye are able; but will with the temptation also make a way to escape, that ye may be able to bear it (1 Cor. 10:13).

I think in this same regard that the worth of a person can always be measured by what happens when he is really facing trouble. It is a given that we will face difficulties and troubles. The pathway to living the crucified life has many obstacles, hindrances and dangers. So it is not that we have these difficulties; rather, it is how we handle those difficulties that really determines the quality of our relationship to God. If we give up, what does that say about our trust in God?

The Example of King David

Nobody had more difficulties and troubles than King David, as recorded in the Old Testament. I am sure that in some instances, he brought some difficulties and problems on himself. But for the most part, his difficulties and burdens were because of God's call on his life.

David recounts these difficulties in Psalm 57. This is a most extraordinary psalm because it gives us a glimpse into the very heart of this man. The quality of David's life is seen in how he faced his difficulty.

In Psalm 57, David confesses the overwhelming nature of his difficulties. In verse 1 he calls them "calamities." It is always good to recognize the problem that is facing you. How many times do people ignore a problem or don't really see the problem in front of them? Nothing is more dangerous than being faced with a problem or difficulty and ignoring it.

David did not ignore his "calamities." He recognized them for what they were. He did not try to explain them away, ignore them or blame someone else for them. That is often what we do when we experience calamities. For some reason, we believe that if we can blame someone else for our problems, the problems will go away. That just doesn't happen.

I do not think there was a cowardly bone in David's body. From the time he faced Goliath until his deathbed, David feared nothing but God. Imagine a teenage boy standing with five smooth stones, facing one of the greatest soldiers of his time. Goliath was a giant in many regards. He was not just big, but he was also a fighting machine. I think it is safe to say that Goliath never lost a battle. His fighting record was tremendous.

That is why the Philistines sent Goliath up in front of the whole Israeli army. They knew what he could do.

However, Goliath had never met David before. Goliath accused David of not knowing what he was doing. He accused him of not understanding what was really at stake. But David told Goliath that he was not coming against him in his own stead but in the name of Jehovah, the God of Israel. As long as David was on God's side, he had nothing whatsoever to fear.

David's encounter with Goliath set a standard for David for the rest of his life.

The Positive Side of Difficulties

There is a positive side to these severe problems and difficulties: Much can be learned by facing them. But we must remember that the enemy facing us, the one attacking us, can discern where we are spiritually and use that against us. Here is the strategy of the enemy. He knows our weak points and attacks them with all the viciousness of hell's fire. But here is what the devil does not know. The apostle Paul points it out for us:

> I take pleasure in infirmities, in reproaches, in necessities, in persecutions, in distresses for Christ's sake: for when I am weak, then am I strong (2 Cor. 12:10).

Those on the journey of living the crucified life know the spiritual dynamic of this statement. It is in our weakness that God manifests Himself so mightily. King David knew that his strength was not in himself but in God.

False Solutions for Our Difficulties

Just as there are many difficulties and problems that we face in our journey, so too there are many solutions. Books by the truckload offer us solutions to one or another of our difficulties and problems. For the most part, however, these books miss the mark.

One solution offered these days is to engage the enemy. When we feel the enemy attacking us, we need to dig in our heels and have a face-off with him. This is a display of spiritual machismo. We want to show the troublemaker, and anybody else who might be watching us, that we're nobody to be fooled with.

The only problem is that the devil will never face you directly. And I might as well say it: The devil does not fight fair. The devil uses rules that he makes up as he goes along. For a Christian to think that he can outguess the devil is probably the most dangerous thought he can harbor.

The devil loves us to engage him in battle. This is what he lives for. He knows that he cannot win, but he also knows that he can do some damage in the process. The entire agenda of the enemy can be boiled down to one objective: embarrass God through some of His children. The devil thought he could do that with Job in the Old Testament. But what the devil did not know was that God was in absolute control every step of the way.

Another solution that some Christians try is using Scripture to defy the enemy. But what these Christians do not realize is that the devil knows Scripture better than some theologians. The devil's heart is not filled with doubt but with hatred and jealousy. His hatred of God and jealousy of God blind him to the reality of God's Lordship.

For any Christian to use Scripture without the Spirit is like engaging in a battle with a paper sword. It is not the Word only that will turn back the devil; rather, it is the Word and the power. The devil can quote Scripture better than any seminary professor, but when the Word is under the direction of the Holy Spirit, it will always find its deadly mark.

The Two-Part Solution for Our Difficulties

When Daniel was thrown into the lions' den, he did nothing to defend himself. He did not try to engage the enemy. He did not try to defy his enemies by quoting Scripture. He simply left his situation in God's hands. This brings me to David's solution to his problems. In Psalm 57, David reveals the only solution to difficulties and problems and calamities. There are two parts to this solution.

Part One: Take Refuge in God

In Psalm 57:1, David says, "In the shadow of thy wings will I make my refuge, until these calamities be overpass." Instead of going out to fight his own battles, David took refuge in God. How tempting it might have been for him to show the enemy his strength and might. To show his enemy that he was not somebody to be messed with must have been a great temptation for a man like David. Instead of engaging the enemy, however, David took refuge in the shadow of God's wings.

What a blessed truth to understand that, in the middle of all of our difficulties and calamities, we have a refuge. Certainly, there is a time to go forth into battle and engage the enemy. But this should only be under the direct orders of the Captain of our salvation. Young David understood this as he faced Goliath.

> And all this assembly shall know that the LORD saveth not with sword and spear: for the battle is the LORD's, and he will give you into our hands (1 Sam. 17:47).

The battle is always the Lord's.

Part Two: Exalt God

The other aspect of David's solution is found in Psalm 57:5. David took refuge in God but, at the same time, he was giving God an opportunity to exalt Himself. "Be thou exalted, O God." This was David's passion. The only way God could be exalted was if he, David, would find his refuge in God.

David was not an opportunist. That is, he did not look for opportunities to exalt himself above the people he was ruling or even to exalt himself above his enemies. Be sure, he had plenty of opportunities along the way to do this.

Although David was not a perfect man, he had a perfect trust in God and not himself. This is where we get into trouble. Certainly, we trust God; but for some reason, we trust ourselves above God, just in case God does not come through. David was not like that. He put himself in such a position that if God did not come through, everything would be lost.

Again, take for example when David faced Goliath. Do you appreciate the great risk David took? I have often wondered why King Saul allowed David to go out there and face Goliath like that. If David had failed, Israel would have failed. The entire situation between Israel and the Philistines boiled down to a teenage boy by the name of David and his five smooth stones and sling. It is hard to imagine David standing in front of the giant. If God did not come through, everything would have been lost for him and the Israelites.

The Language of Heaven

It boils down to this: Are you willing to say, "Oh, Lord, exalt Yourself above me and all that I am—possessions, friends, comforts, pleasures, reputation, health and life—everything. Test me, Lord, and see whether I can really leave everything in Your hands. Bring my life into line so that I will not be fully myself, but fully in You, knowing the truth that I can take refuge in You."

If you have come this far, may I suggest one further step in your prayer: "Oh, Lord, set in motion a chain of circumstances that will bring me to the place where I can sincerely say, 'Be thou exalted above the heavens.'"

Have you ever wondered what language they speak in heaven? This is it. This is the language of heaven. They will come from the north and the south and east and the west. They will come from German, Spanish, Greek and Syrian speaking countries. They will come from all around the world and will never have to sit down and go through the process of learning a new language. In the kingdom of God, everyone will speak the same language of which the keynote will be: "Worthy is the Lamb that was slain to receive glory and power and wisdom and might and honor" (see Rev. 4:11). You will know heaven's language when you get there without having to study it—and you will not speak with an accent.

Allowing yourself to be put in such a position that God is exalted is the goal of living the crucified life. When you allow God to be exalted in your difficulties, you will be in the perfect position to smell the sweet fragrance of His presence.

All Hail the Power of Jesus' Name
Edward Perronet (1726–1792)

All hail the power of Jesus' name!
Let angels prostrate fall;
Bring forth the royal diadem,
And crown Him Lord of all;
Bring forth the royal diadem,
And crown Him Lord of all.

Ye chosen seed of Israel's race,
Ye ransomed from the fall,

Hail Him who saves you by His grace,
And crown Him Lord of all;
Hail Him who saves you by His grace,
And crown Him Lord of all.

Sinners, whose love can never forget
The wormwood and the gall,
Go spread your trophies at His feet,
And crown Him Lord of all;
Go spread your trophies at His feet,
And crown Him Lord of all.

Let every kindred, every tribe,
On this terrestrial ball,
To Him all majesty ascribe,
And crown Him Lord of all;
To Him all majesty ascribe,
And crown Him Lord of all.

O that with yonder sacred throng,
We at His feet may fall!
We'll join the everlasting song,
And crown Him Lord of all;
We'll join the everlasting song,
And crown Him Lord of all.

Crown him, ye morning stars of light,
Who fixed this earthly ball;
Now hail the strength of Israel's might,
And crown Him Lord of all,
Now hail the strength of Israel's might,
And crown Him Lord of all.

16

SPIRITUAL GUIDES
FOR THE JOURNEY

And I will give you pastors according to mine heart, which shall feed
you with knowledge and understanding.

JEREMIAH 3:15

The way of the crucified life can be precarious, making a spiritual guide all but indispensable. But it is important to have a guide who understands the way sufficiently and can give clear instructions on how to live the crucified life. The Church has no shortage of people who have advice to give. There is, however, a shortage of spiritual guides with the wisdom needed to navigate such precarious living. The question to be considered is, how do you recognize a true spiritual guide?

It is crucial that we watch out for the false guides. For every true guide there are a multitude of false ones. The use of false guides is a popular strategy of the enemy to destroy the work of God in a person's life. Some guides are obviously false and easily recognized as such because their teachings are completely off-the-wall. What I am concerned about, however, are those false guides who are close to the truth.

One of the first things that should catch our attention about a potential guide is his use of Scripture. The most dangerous spiritual guide is the person who is 95 percent true to the Scriptures. Remember, it is not the truth that hurts you; rather, it is the evil. The 95-percent truth is trumped by the 5 percent of evil. This our archenemy knows only too well.

The true spiritual guide embraces all of the Scriptures, while the false guide will avoid certain passages of Scripture. This is something only the well-taught Christian can fully recognize. Unfortunately, the problem today is that many Christians are not well versed in the teachings of Scripture.

Another sign that should concern us is the use of extra-scriptural material. Many of these false guides will begin with some Scripture and gradually move into some extra-scriptural material. It might be a book or series of essays or some poetry. What it is makes no difference. Everything must be tested by the Word of God, which is the final authority for the Christian. The place of the Bible in someone's teaching should clue us in to the genuineness of a spiritual guide.

One more sign of false spiritual guides is their undue emphasis upon themselves. When the teaching always focuses on the teacher, that is a clue that something is wrong. The true spiritual guide will focus all of the teaching on Jesus Christ and only on the Christ of the Bible.

True Spiritual Guides

Most of the true spiritual guides are what I refer to as "evangelical mystics." I know the terminology is not acceptable in many Christian circles, so let me explain a little of what I mean. By "evangelical mystic," I mean someone who has his feet firmly and irrevocably planted in the Scriptures. This is the absolute first qualification of true spiritual guides. They have accepted the Scriptures as their only rule for faith and practice and have put their faith and trust in the Lord Jesus Christ of the Bible. I do not need any suppositions mixed with airy speculations. I want to know that my spiritual guide is committed to the Word of God.

Diagnose the Inner Spiritual Life

There are several other aspects of these spiritual guides that are important. First, true spiritual guides are what I would call soul surgeons who possess the power to diagnose the inner spiritual life. Traveling down the crucified life pathway, we certainly are in need of a physician of the soul who can trace with great skill our heart's troubles. Spiritual diagnosis is very valuable in maintaining solid spiritual health. It is one thing to diagnose a problem and something else altogether to prescribe a cure based on Scripture and not on worldly wisdom.

The wisdom of this world has nothing to offer the heart cry of the soul infatuated with God. All of the feel-good therapy can in no way touch the inner reaches of the soul. We need a spiritual guide who knows God, knows the Word of God and understands human nature.

Practice the Inward Life

Effective spiritual guides will be apostles of the inward life without ever succumbing to being merely introspective. They probe the interior reaches of the soul so that they may turn the inner eye outward, focusing upon the person of Christ. Their goal is to lead the soul upward into the wonderment that is God.

Exude Fresh Spirituality

What makes these spiritual guides so refreshing is their spiritual originality. In reading some of their works, you will catch a sense of the freshness of the dew of God's presence upon them. They do not just write a collection of words to produce copy but powerful words that produce in the heart of the man who longs for God a fragrance of God's presence. In reading these works, we have a sense that we are encountering the words of a true seer, someone who knows whereof he speaks.

We are so accustomed these days to reading books written by authors who copied from other books ad nausea. Such books have the musty smell of mindless repetition and spiritual bankruptcy. When we come to the literature by these spiritual guides, we quickly sense the difference. There is no repetition of religious ideology here but rather a sacred revelation of the heart and mind of God based upon the sacred Scriptures.

Experience the Same Difficulties that We Have

The thing that makes true spiritual guides so genuine is the fact that they live real lives and encounter real difficulties. Many of them were martyrs for the cause of Christ and left behind proof of their incredible devotion to God. They knew what it meant to suffer hardship for the cause of Christ. They did not live in ivory towers sheltered from the harshness and bitterness of the world's opposition to true spirituality. Many of them found themselves in exile because of their commitment to the inner way. Their ways were not easy and strewn with roses, but there was a fragrance of God's presence, which for them made all the difference in the world.

Devoted Exclusively to God

True spiritual guides are men and women who are devoted to God exclusively. Their lives are not dependent on human reason, imagination and feeling. Nor are they caught up in talking eloquently about divine things and spewing glowing thoughts about God that are far removed from the average Christian. They have discovered the simplicity of fellowship and solitude with God.

Hate Evil

The mark of devotion these men and women have are a common horror of evil and sin. Nothing so stirs their rage as the evil around them, particularly the evil in the Church. Nothing so stirs their imagination as thoughts of God and His kingdom within. They cultivate within themselves a perpetual habit of listening to that sweet inner voice of His presence. Out of such inner experiences comes a radical determination to obey that voice, regardless of the cost.

The Literature of Past Spiritual Guides

The literature of these evangelical mystics and spiritual guides focuses on the worshiper rather than the student. Everything is prepared for those God-enamored people who seek God above all other things and who disdain the things of this world.

The poetry of these evangelical mystics soars into the heavens above with such rapturous joy and delightful harmony with the divine. Reading the poetry of these spiritual guides is to experience their passion for God. Often after reading such poetry, I lay the book down and sigh deeply within, satisfied with the wonderful truth that the writer was able to express my deepest feelings for God in language far better than my ability to compose.

Whether reading a book of essays or poems, one must keep in mind that it was never intended to be used in public. These works were meant to be read in the privacy of personal worship. Surrounded by the solitude of adoring wonder, these authors lift our hearts in joyous anticipation of the manifest presence of God.

With all of that said, however, I need to set forth some guidelines for reading some of these great books of spiritual devotion. Never come to one of these books as you would come to another type of literature. Too many people in their rush to finish the reading miss out on the quiet of experiencing the presence of God. Some of these books will take you places you've never been before spiritually.

Come with a Spirit of Longing

The first thing to keep in mind when reading one of these Christian devotional classics is to come with the spirit of longing. Those with a strong sense of curiosity need not read these books. There will be nothing to satiate their curiosity. These classics demand that the reader come with a strong desire to know God. Without that strong desire, the reader will quickly tire and grow bored with the book. Nothing is here for the frivolous of heart. Nothing is here to entertain the mature Christian. Everything here stirs up an insatiable desire to know God in the fullness of His revelation. When this is done, the whole inner life will be quickened and enriched by truth.

Come After Praying and Meditating on the Scriptures

Another recommendation would be in the area of prayer. Only come to such books after significant time in prayer and meditation on the Scriptures. Anyone who comes unprepared and hurriedly will miss the whole intent of these books. If our hearts are not prepared to receive, our time in these books will not be time well spent.

This is one of the major things wrong with today's Christian Church. In our hurry to keep up with the culture around us, we have reserved little time to quietly wait before God and meditate on His Word. The reader who prepares his heart and mind to receive will experience in these classics vistas of glorious revelation of God.

Have a Devotional Attitude

Another thing has to do with our attitude. It is very difficult to find time, let alone intention, to quietly wait before the Lord. But when we come to one of these great spiritual classics, we need to come with an attitude of devotion. This is hard for us as Americans. We rush here and there with an energy that can't last forever. Then we collapse in a heap of exhaustion.

To get the most out of these books, it is important for us to learn how to develop the disciplines of silence and meditation. The world is too much among us. We need to learn how to shake it off and worthily come into the presence of almighty God. I believe that humbling ourselves in silence before God will create within us a real spirit of expectation of what we really expect God to do in and through this book that we have before us. That is why I said earlier that these books are not for public reading. These books are for a person to get alone and read quietly, slowly and meditatively. Getting away from all distractions will go a long way in developing the discipline of concentration on the things of God.

Surrender and Consecrate Yourself

Before beginning to read one of these classics, it is important that you make sure you have surrendered and consecrated yourself to God. The spiritual guides begin where others leave off. The assumption from their point of view is that you are ready to go further into the deep things of God, that you are already starting to live the crucified life. So before you begin to read, spend time alone with God and get your heart in such a submissive and obedient position that God can begin speaking to you through the voices of these spiritual guides.

If there are large areas of your life that remain unsurrendered to Christ, the reading of these books will benefit you quite little. Get the surrendering done. These works are all intended to help the pilgrim along the way, but you must already be started along the correct path.

Be Earnest

Another important aspect is to come with a sense of earnestness. These writers assume that the readers are serious. They are not writing to satisfy the curiosity of those who have no earnest intention of putting into practice the teaching. These books are for the souls of those who thirst for God—and only God. The books will not entertain you. None of them were written with entertainment or amusement in mind.

I have read many of these books and I have never found any of them to be fun. Each one has taken me deeper or higher into the presence of God, and the way is not an easy one. It is not for the fainthearted. Rather, it is for those who want to know God and care not about the price. There is no "fun" in these books, but you can be sure there will be plenty of glory for those who pursue their teachings in earnest.

Read Slowly

Another point needs to be established here. I highly recommend that you never read more than one chapter in a day. It is impossible to hurry through these books and receive the full benefit that they possess. Slow down, meditate long and hard on each and every chapter, paragraph, sentence and, yes, even word. These books are to be studied, meditated on, marked up, prayed over and read as long as they continue to minister to the soul.

Assemble a Library

There are in Christian literature those books that can be read once and then forgotten. Sir Francis Bacon wrote, "Some books are to be tasted, others to be swallowed, and some few to be chewed and digested: that is, some books are to be read only in parts, others to be read, but not curiously, and some few to be read wholly, and with diligence and attention." These great Christian classics fall under the last category.

I highly recommend assembling a library of these books to be read and meditated on for the rest of your life. It seems highly improbable to me that anybody would ever outgrow the richness found in these volumes.

The journey is rough. The path we have to tread is one filled with danger and trouble in difficulties. Only a trustworthy guide can help us along the way and enable us with great victory to live the crucified life.

Hiding in Thee
William O. Cushing

O safe to the Rock that is higher than I,
My soul in its conflicts and sorrows would fly;
So sinful, so weary, Thine, Thine, would I be;
Thou blest "Rock of Ages," I'm hiding in Thee.

Hiding in Thee, hiding in Thee,
Thou blest "Rock of Ages,"
I'm hiding in Thee.

In the calm of the noontide, in sorrow's lone hour,
In times when temptation casts o'er me its power;
In the tempests of life, on its wide, heaving sea,
Thou blest "Rock of Ages," I'm hiding in Thee.

How oft in the conflict, when pressed by the foe,
I have fled to my refuge and breathed out my woe;
How often, when trials like sea billows roll,
Have I hidden in Thee, O Thou Rock of my soul.

THE PURPOSE OF THE REFINER'S FIRE IN THE CRUCIFIED LIFE

*If it be so, our God whom we serve is able to deliver
us from the burning fiery furnace, and he will deliver
us out of thine hand, O king. But if not, be it known
unto thee, O king, that we will not serve thy gods, nor
worship the golden image which thou hast set up.*

DANIEL 3:17-18

God has in His arsenal an infinite number of tools that He at His discretion employs to accomplish His perfect purpose in our life. Of course, the prevailing question is, what is God's purpose in our lives? The answer to that one question will open up a whole world of understanding concerning what God is doing in our circumstances.

Some have the idea that God's purpose is to make our lives more tolerable here on earth. That rather cheapens what Christ did on the cross. If all He wanted to do was make our lives tolerable, then He could have done it in a variety of other ways. God's supreme purpose for us is to make us like His Son, Jesus Christ. If we understand that everything happening to us is to make us more Christlike, it will solve a great deal of anxiety in our lives.

If, on the other hand, we have the idea that God's purpose is to make this life heaven on earth, then God has a lot of explaining to do. It is not happening. The way is rough, and the pathway is littered with all kinds of distractions and disturbances along the way.

Throughout this book, I have referred to the cross as an instrument to accomplish God's purpose, His ultimate purpose in our life. I now want to refer to another tool that goes along with this: the Refiner's Fire. Let me point out the difference between these two. The cross deals with our self-life; to put self on the cross and have it absolutely crucified under Christ. But the Refiner's Fire takes a different approach. The purpose of the Refiner's Fire is to burn away all the bondage imposed on us by the world.

When I talk about "the world," I am not referring to the mountains and valleys and the meadows and the forest. I am talking about the spirit of this world that is diametrically opposed to everything that God represents. The spirit of this world is supervised by none other than the enemy of our soul, even Satan himself, which the Scriptures refer to as the "prince of the power of the air" (Eph. 2:2). The apostle Paul also refers to him as the god of this world:

> In whom the god of this world hath blinded the minds of them which believe not, lest the light of the glorious gospel of Christ, who is the image of God, should shine unto them (2 Cor. 4:4).

Even as God the Father did not spare His own Son the pains and the sufferings of the cross, so too God will not spare us any pain in bringing us to that ultimate place of Christlikeness. As the author of Hebrews states:

> For whom the Lord loveth he chasteneth, and scourgeth every son whom he receiveth. If ye endure chastening, God dealeth with you as with sons; for what son is he whom the father chasteneth not? (Heb. 12:6-7).

A casual perusal of the Scriptures will bring one to the conclusion that God is never in a rut. For the most part, He rarely repeats Himself. There was only one Daniel in the lions' den; only once did three Hebrew children get cast into the fiery furnace; and God only appeared once in a burning bush to a man. God, in His infinite wisdom and at His complete discretion, deals with His people to bring them to His appointed place.

The Refiner's Fire is simply an instrument by which God accomplishes His purposes in our lives. We are never to worship fire. Remember that Israel fell into idolatry by worshiping the brazen serpent that stopped the death angel. The brazen serpent was only to remind them of what God had done, but they became more enamored with the object than the God behind the object. We are to allow God to use whatever instrument or tool He chooses to accomplish His purpose. Again, that purpose is to bring us to a point of absolute Christlikeness, because it is through the Son that He is glorified.

To understand God and His nature is to understand that nothing impure can stand before Him. Therefore, in dealing with us as sons and daughters, we must meet His standard of purity. Nothing impure, nothing from this world, nothing contrary to the nature and character of God can be left in our lives. Some aspects of our lives are so resistant to God's grace that it necessitates fire to burn it completely out of our lives.

Requirements of the Crucified Life

In Daniel 3, we read the story of the Babylonian king Nebuchadnezzar who had an image of gold made and ordered all of the people in his kingdom to bow down and worship it. When Shadrach, Meshach and Abednego—men who served the Lord—refused to bow to the image, the king had them thrown into a fiery furnace. The actions of these three Hebrew children reveal several aspects that are crucial to living the crucified life.

Obedience

First, Shadrach, Meshach and Abednego were obedient to the Lord. Obedience is a primary component of the Christian life. Note that their obedience did not require them to know why this situation was happening to them, nor did it require God to do everything according to their understanding. I am sure they had no idea of why all of a sudden the tables had been turned on them. They had been good servants of Nebuchadnezzar, and he had honored them by placing them in positions of authority. Now everything seemed to be going against them.

As you think of this story, keep in mind that their obedience to God was what got them in trouble in the first place. It was the door into the furnace. As I have previously mentioned, somewhere along the line Christians have developed the idea that if they obey God it will keep them out of trouble. Yet that is not the purpose of obedience. In looking at the lives of the men and women of the Old and New Testaments, and even throughout Church history, we find that it was obedience that often got them into difficulties.

I referred earlier to Dietrich Bonhoeffer. His obedience sent him straight to the gallows. He could have escaped, but it would have required him to compromise his relationship to God, which was something he would never have thought of doing.

True obedience is the refusal to compromise in any regard our relationship with God, regardless of the consequences.

Keep in mind that the god of this world does not mind if you believe in God. "Thou believest that there is one God; thou doest well: the devils also believe, and tremble" (Jas. 2:19). The devil believes in God, so you are on the same page as him. He does not even mind if you worship God, provided you also worship the gods of this world. As long as you believe in God as millions of Americans do today and do not make Him the number one exclusive priority in your life, the devil has no issue with you. The evangelical church today is following the course of the liberal movement and going down the same pathway of compromise. One compromise here, another compromise there, and soon there is very little, if any, difference between the so-called Christian and the man in the world.

True obedience, as illustrated in the story of the three Hebrew children, always brings us to a point of no return. This is where faith comes in. We do not have to understand what is happening in order to obey God. We do not need to know the outcome in order to obey God. As a matter of faith and trust, we obey God simply because He is God. This obedience brings us to a point of a personal resolution where we do not have to be delivered from our trouble.

Obedience is recognizing God's sovereignty and authority and submitting to it without question and without regard to consequence. We see this aspect of complete obedience in the lives of Shadrach, Meshach and Abednego when they said, "Our God whom we serve is able to deliver us from the burning fiery furnace . . . but if not, be it known unto thee, O king, that we will not serve thy gods, nor worship the golden image which thou hast set up" (Dan. 3:17-18). Their obedience did not depend on God rescuing them from a hard place. They knew He could, but if He did not rescue them, it had no bearing upon their absolute obedience to God.

Surrender

The three Hebrew children's absolute obedience to God brought them to a place of ultimate surrender to the situation at hand. We do not like to talk about this. We want to talk about God delivering us from hard places so we can say, "Glory to God, He rescued me." But surrender means nothing of the sort.

The essence of surrender is getting out of the way so that God can do what He wants to do. So often we are in a position that God cannot do His work. Then we stand around wondering why nothing is happening. Nothing is happening because we are standing obstinate to God in refusing to surrender to the situation at hand.

Nebuchadnezzar was kind enough to give the three Hebrew children an opportunity to reconsider their position. After all, the world's philosophy is that you have to give a little to get a little. He tried to make it easy for them. In the natural, they were in a position where their allegiance to Nebuchadnezzar would have gone a long way toward helping the people of Israel. It would only have cost them a little compromise here or there. That is how the world works, but it is not how it works in God's kingdom.

One thing the three Hebrew children understood was who was supreme ruler in this world. Nebuchadnezzar thought so highly of himself, but he posed no threat to these Jewish men whose allegiance and loyalty was to God alone. Some would have us believe that by surrendering to a situation we are exercising a cowardly act. The only person who would buy into that philosophy is one who does not know the ways of God. While it is true that there are times when we need to stand against a certain situation or problem—when repudiating the situation is the order of the day—we must never confuse that with an opportunity to surrender in such a way that we get out of God's way and allow Him to do in us what He wants to do through us.

The furnace represented the worst the world could do. In fact, Nebuchadnezzar was so angry with these Jewish men that he ordered the furnace turned up seven times hotter than before. Then he commanded these Jewish men to be bound and cast into the fiery furnace. As Shadrach, Meshach and Abednego surrendered to the flames of that furnace, they were stepping into God's arena.

I note with a great deal of satisfaction that Nebuchadnezzar's men, whose job it was to throw these Jewish men into the fiery furnace, were the only ones consumed by that fire. In fact, the only thing the flames consumed was Nebuchadnezzar's men and the Hebrew children's bonds. That which was of the world, Nebuchadnezzar and the bonds, were absolutely consumed by the flame of that furnace. But nothing of God's was ever harmed.

> And the princes, governors, and captains, and the king's counsellors, being gathered together, saw these men, upon whose bodies the fire had no power, nor was an hair of their head singed, neither were their coats changed, nor the smell of fire had passed on them (Dan. 3:27).

I do not see why the world has any attraction for anyone. Anybody who can read anything about history will understand that the world always destroys its own. Joshua understood this when he told the Israelites, "If it seem evil unto you to serve the LORD, choose you this day whom ye will serve; whether the gods which your fathers served that were on the other side of the flood, or the gods of the Amorites, in whose land ye dwell: but as for me and my house, we will serve the LORD" (Josh. 24:15). If you want to follow the god of this world, Joshua said, then go for it. But, as he testified with great confidence, he and his house would serve the Lord. He understood that the world always turns on its own.

Nebuchadnezzar's men were destroyed because the three Hebrew children obeyed God and surrendered to the furnace. How in the world can you defeat such men as these? How can you threaten them into submission? The flame had caused no damage to them at all. That was the astonishing thing as far as Nebuchadnezzar was concerned. That which he had designed to destroy God's men had backfired and only destroyed his men.

If only we could get this into our head. If only we could truly believe that God has an agenda in this world and that we are part of that agenda. Although the circumstances of our life are opportunities for God to defeat the world, the only thing standing in the way is the hesitant Christian demanding that God rescue him from any trouble. But it is trouble that enables God to get the glory.

The same flame that consumed the natural world and the bondage imposed by the world on the Christian is the same flame that purifies the Christian. The fire burns out the impurities and brings the gold to a state of purification. The more intense the flame, the purer the gold.

Revelation

Thus, if we desire to live the crucified life, we must completely submit in obedience to the Lord and surrender our lives to God's authority so that He can do His work. Once we are out of His way, He then has the opportunity to reveal Himself to us and to the world around us as in no other way. Often, the only way the world can see Christ is through revelation brought by the Christian's experience in the Refiner's Fire.

After Shadrach, Meshach and Abednego had been thrown into the flames, Nebuchadnezzar looked into that furnace and saw something he never expected to see. He thought these flames that he had built would consume the men. Instead, not only did he see them alive and unharmed, but he also saw a fourth man in the furnace.

> Then Nebuchadnezzar the king was astonished, and rose up in haste, and spake, and said unto his counsellors, Did not we cast three men bound into the midst of the fire? They answered and said unto the king, True, O king. He answered and said, Lo, I see four men loose, walking in the midst of the fire, and they have no hurt; and the form of the fourth is like the Son of God (Dan. 3:24-25).

Oh, see that fourth man in the flame! That is the revelation of God. What does it take to experience God in this way? It takes a furnace. It takes obedience to God and submitting to Him in absolute surrender. That is all.

The Joy of God's Presence

The fire in the furnace reveals Christ in the midst of His people, sharing their fellowship. The flame of Nebuchadnezzar's furnace did not overcome the fragrance of God's presence. Imagine the joy of those men in the flames. There is no joy comparable to that joy of being in a place where God joins you in sweet fellowship. Never in the marketplace. Never on the mountaintop. Remember Peter on the Mount of Transfiguration. He wanted to set up a couple of tents, forget the rest of the world and enjoy fellowship with God. But the value of the mountaintop experience is revealed in the valley below in which we must tread.

The revelation of God is the fruit of the flame. How many times have we missed the fragrance of God's presence because we resist the furnace and the tribulation and the suffering before us? We have it all worked out. We read a couple of verses of Scripture and say, "I believe." That settles it. We think we can then go on our merry way to heaven, whistling "When the Saints Come Marching In." We want to be coddled on our way to heaven and have an easy life. We want to make sure that we are going to go to heaven when we die, but in the meantime we want to enjoy the pleasures of the world.

There is no revelation of God in following that path. There is no experiencing the fragrance of God's presence. There is no burning of the bonds that the world has imposed upon us, setting us free to follow our Lord. Yes, we walk by faith. But occasionally there are some glorious moments in which God reveals Himself to us. I tell you, this is holy ground. This is an area of sacredness incomparable to anything else this side of glory.

Keep in mind that God has a vision for us beyond the furnace. The fires serve its purpose, burning away the bonds of the world and purifying our relationship with God, and then we move on. Shadrach, Meshach and Abednego walked out of that furnace. Imagine the testimony they would have the rest of their lives. They certainly were creatures out of the fire. They were men who had met God in the wondrous, glorious fashion incomparable to anything else in their lives. They were counted worthy to suffer for Christ.

If we are ever going to see God in the fullness of His manifestation, we must be like these men. We must obey Him implicitly and surrender in such a way that He can place us where He wants to place us in order to show us what He wants to show us. And what He does to us He will also do through us to confound the wisdom of the world, who cannot figure out what we are.

God's most delicate tools are reserved for His special children. For the Christian on the path of the crucified life, God will bring into his pathway the fiery furnace, the Refiner's Fire, and show that Christian how much He really loves him.

Nothing Between My Soul and the Savior
Charles Albert Tindley (1851–1933)

Nothing between my soul and the Savior,
Naught of this world's delusive dream;
I have renounced all sinful pleasure;
Jesus is mine, there's nothing between.

Nothing between my soul and the Savior,
So that His blessed face may be seen;
Nothing preventing the least of His favor,
Keep the way clear! Let nothing between.

Nothing between, like worldly pleasure;
Habits of life, though harmless they seem,
Must not my heart from Him e'er sever;
He is my all, there's nothing between.

Nothing between, like pride or station;
Self-life or friends shall not intervene;
Though it may cost me much tribulation,
I am resolved; there's nothing between.

Nothing between, e'en many hard trials,
Though the whole world against me convene;
Watching with prayer and much self-denial,
I'll triumph at last, with nothing between.

Follow Tozer's new writings on Twitter at
http://twitter.com/tozeraw

EXCERPTS FROM

INSPIRED BY
TOZER

• •

A NEW BOOK FEATURING MORE THAN
50 INSPIRATIONAL READINGS FROM WRITERS,
ARTISTS AND LEADERS SUCH AS:
LISA BEVERE, CHUCK SWINDOLL,
KURT WARNER, BEN KASICA (OF SKILLET),
RANDY ALCORN, RAVI ZACHARIAS,
BRITT NICOLE, KENNETH ULMER AND MORE

• •

LAUREN BARLOW, GENERAL EDITOR

Saying Yes to the Unknown

Lauren Barlow

Drummer and Singer, BarlowGirl

*Faith never asks questions when it has been established that
God has spoken. Thus faith honors God by counting Him righteous
and accepts his testimony against the very evidence of his own senses.
This is faith, and of such we can never have too much.*

A.W. Tozer

The summer of 1999 is one I will never forget. It all started
when my mom came to our family during our prayer time and
said she felt God had shown her the verse in Luke 5:4 where Jesus says to Peter, "Put out into deep water, and let down your
nets for a catch" (*NIV*).

That's all He gave her—nothing more. No explanation. Nothing. But somehow she felt that God was asking our family to
get ready—to get ready for something big, whatever it may be.

Now, as a 14-year-old, I really had no clue what to expect.
Quite frankly, I have never been very partial to fishing, and I
wanted nothing to do with that. But, of course, I didn't want to
let my dislike of fishing get in the way of something God was
trying to say to my family, so, trying to be good a Christian family, we said, "Yes God, we will get ready for whatever it is You
have for us, no matter what."

Saying yes to the unknown with God can be a very scary
thing.

What in the world had we just said yes to? We honestly had no clue. But we were a family who always tried to say yes to God, because we knew He was always looking for people who were willing to do anything for Him. We wanted to be those people. Little did we know that less than 12 hours later we would get a phone call that would answer all of our questions from that morning.

My dad received that phone call from a ministry called World Relief. World Relief is a non-profit organization that helps victims of poverty, disease, hunger, war, disasters and persecution. About a month earlier, my dad had called them to ask if there was any way we could get involved with their organization or help in any way. He hadn't heard back from them until now.

The people at World Relief informed my dad that they were involved with helping all the refugees that were coming over to America because of the war happening in Kosovo. Many Kosovars were being sent out of the refugee camps and out of the country because it was too dangerous for them to stay there. I'm sure my dad was wondering where the conversation was going. Then they asked him the big question: "There are 14 Kosovars on a plane to Chicago right now. They aren't supposed to be coming to Chicago, but their flight got messed up so they are stuck. No church will take them because there are too many of them. So, since you recently asked if you could help, do you want to take them in? They will be here first thing in the morning."

My dad asked if he could call them back. He wanted to talk it all over with us first before he committed to doing anything. So he asked my mom what she thought, and of course mom said without hesitating, *"Yes! Send them all to us!"* Then they asked us kids whether that would be okay, and we all said yes. So dad called World Relief back five minutes later and told him we would take in all 14 people.

Now, let me share a little background with you. Bottom line, we weren't exactly wealthy. We didn't have some huge house that 14 people could stay in. We lived in a four-bedroom house. Four bedrooms. Fourteen people. (Well, 19 if you count my family and me.) Also, Dad had just quit his job to start a family ministry, so technically we were self-employed. Oh, and did I mention that none of us knew a word of Albanian and they didn't know a word of English? It's true.

If you looked at this situation in the natural, you would have thought we were absolutely crazy. Honestly, when people heard what we were doing, they thought that exact thing. But our family knew that when God calls you to do something, you can never look at it through your natural eyes. If we had tried to figure things out in our heads, we would have just messed up what God was trying to do. Something we all have to know is that God will never call us to do something and then forget to walk us through the process. Even though it sometimes feels as though we are walking blindly, God is always walking with us to the end.

If I took the time to share with you every miracle that we saw happen during those two months we had with the Behluli family from Kosovo, it would fill an entire book. But I will tell you that God provided abundantly more than we could have ever asked for. For two months there was food, clothing, toys, electronics, free doctor visits and free housing for all 14 of them—and anything and everything else we could ever want. Most of it just ended up right on our doorstep.

The family came to us with nothing. Literally, all their bags were lost when they flew here, and they left us with three suitcases each. We could hardly understand each other, but we still spent every waking moment of that summer together. Somehow, there was an understanding.

That was 12 years ago. We haven't seen the Behlulis since they left us. But every time I look back on that summer, I am reminded of God's goodness. And I think of how sad it would have been if we hadn't had the faith to say yes to God. We would have missed out on so much.

That's what faith is all about.

So step out. Go out into the deep and get ready to catch something, even if you aren't that crazy about fishing. Because you never know what amazing things God has for you when you have the faith to simply say yes.

To Find God's Will, Do God's Will

Gregg Matte

SENIOR PASTOR, FIRST BAPTIST CHURCH, HOUSTON, TEXAS
FOUNDER, BREAKAWAY MINISTRIES AT TEXAS A&M UNIVERSITY

The man or woman who is wholly or joyously surrendered to Christ can't make a wrong choice. Any choice will be the right one.
A.W. TOZER

We know where Moses was when God called to him. We know how old he was and what his past held. But maybe more important than any of these things is what Moses was doing when he encountered the burning bush: *nothing remarkable*. He was tending his father-in-law's flock, like he had done every day for half his life or more. Shepherding was his regular routine, and he was faithfully doing his job. Leading the flock to this area of the mountain was undoubtedly not a special occasion for Moses but something he did regularly, for shepherds often moved their flocks as the seasons changed and grazing conditions varied. He had almost certainly been on the backside of this mountain before.

Did you notice that Moses didn't even have his own sheep? They belonged to his father-in-law. Nothing remarkable there, for sure; he was on the backside of a mountain watching someone else's flock. But somehow he was ripe for God's choosing. The stage was being set. This was going to be a day of unexpected change. The hinge was about to swing on the "before" and "after" of Moses' life.

Today could be that same kind of day for you. God is not looking to elevate the already elevated. He is looking to tell a story—a story of the greatness of His plan, not a story about our skill. This week, a relational intersection could change the course of your life. A conversation on bended knee could be the tipping point of your prayer life. By the same token, an unexpected phone call could bring you to your knees in grief. Life isn't always easy, and its course can change in seconds, even as we try to plan out the years. What Jesus said in Matthew 6:34 is true: "Do not worry about tomorrow, for tomorrow will worry about itself. Each day has enough trouble of its own" (*NIV*).

Often we imagine that God's will is "out there" somewhere, 90 miles ahead of us and hidden like a needle in a haystack. But for Moses it was very close and not hidden at all. Each step tending his father-in-law's sheep in Nowheresville was a step closer to discovery. In fact, God helped him see it by calling attention to it, just in case he might have passed it by. He caused an ordinary bush to burn in an attention-getting way and appeared to Moses within the flame, calling him by name.

You might say, "I'd stop too if I saw a little self-starting bonfire like that, or if I heard God audibly speak my name." But would you, like Moses, be faithful in doing the thing that God puts before you to do when He calls?

The best way to *find* the will of God is to *do* the will of God. Let me offer an example to bring this home. How do you find God's will for career endeavors? First, you walk with integrity in all your dealings at work and you walk with a generous heart. You offer grace and understanding to your co-workers and colleagues, knowing that human beings make mistakes and that we're all in need of God's grace. When you walk out your faith each day at work in a godly fashion, you'll find that God will arrive before you do and show you the next step to take. Hard work and honesty are always in demand, regardless of the economy. Being the kind of employee that employers dream of puts usable material in the Lord's hands. He is the best agent a faithful job hunter can hope for.

How do you find someone to marry or improve your existing marriage? You walk with purity, as the Bible teaches. You become the kind of person you want to be married to. Are you looking for someone kind? Then grow in kindness. Are you looking for someone responsible? Then pay your bills on time. Are you looking for your spouse to be a person of prayer? Then hit your knees. Become the person to whom you want to be married. Godliness is not a luxury or a bonus in a dating relationship or marriage (see 2 Cor. 6:14); it's a requirement. If you are a Christian and intend to obey God and marry a Christian, then you need to be dating a Christ-follower. If you are married and desire greater godliness in you spouse, step it up yourself. By doing God's will, you take a step further in finding His will. A German proverb sums it up: "Begin to weave, and God will give you the thread."

Too many times we stand dead still at a fork in the road, refusing to move and pleading for God to show us the way. But He is saying, "If you will just walk with Me, I will show you." The best way to *find* the will of God is to *do* the will of God. Mark Twain is alleged to have once said, "It ain't those parts of the Bible that I can't understand that bother me, it is the parts that I do understand." We already know much in our core about what is right and what is wrong. By living what we know, God is preparing us to live what we don't yet know. We can't do multiplication until we learn addition.

We prepare for the future by doing the next right thing. As Tommy Nelson says, "God hits moving targets." Doing God's will leads to discovering God's will. Each step on the mountainside of faith is a step closer to your burning bush. Even if you have someone else's sheep in tow on the far side of town, God may have a life-changing intersection for you just around the next bend.

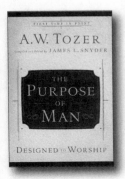
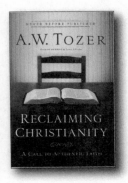
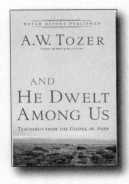
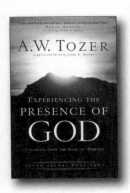
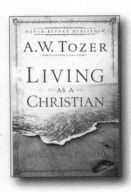
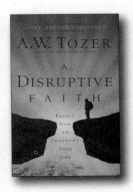

A.W. TOZER:
THE AUTHORIZED BIOGRAPHY

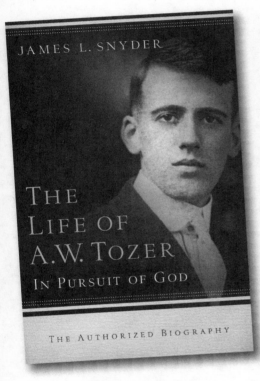

THE LIFE OF A.W. TOZER
IN PURSUIT OF GOD
James L. Snyder
ISBN 978.08307.46941
ISBN 08307.46943

To understand the ministry of A.W. Tozer, it is important to know who he was, including his relationship with God. In *The Life of A.W. Tozer,* James L. Snyder lets us in on the life and times of a deep thinker who was not afraid to "tell it like it is" and never compromised his beliefs. A.W. Tozer's spiritual legacy continues today as his writings challenge readers to a deeper relationship and worship of God in reverence and adoration. Here is Tozer's life story, from boyhood to his conversion at the age of 17, to his years of pastoring and writing more than 40 books (at least two of which are regarded as Christian classics and continue to appear on bestseller lists today). Examining Tozer's life will allow you to learn from a prophet who had much to say against the compromises he observed in contemporary Christian living and the hope he found in his incredible God.